T0271513

Shen Gong and Nei Dan in Da Xuan

of related interest

Warrior Guards the Mountain
The Internal Martial Traditions of China, Japan and South East Asia
Alex Kozma
ISBN 978 1 84819 124 2
eISBN 978 0 85701 101 5

Tranquil Sitting
A Taoist Journal on Meditation and Chinese Medical Qigong
Yin Shi Zi
Forewords by Master Zhongxian Wu and Glenn H. Mullin
Translated by Shi Fu Hwang and Cheney Crow
ISBN 978 1 84819 112 9
eISBN 978 0 85701 090 2

The Key to the Qigong Meditation State
Rujing and Still Qigong
Tianjun Liu, O.M.D.
Foreword by Master Zhongxian Wu
ISBN 978 1 84819 232 4
eISBN 978 0 85701 177 0

Daoist Nei Gong
The Philosophical Art of Change
Damo Mitchell
Foreword by Dr Cindy Engel
ISBN 978 1 84819 065 8
eISBN 978 0 85701 033 9

SHEN GONG
and NEI DAN
in DA XUAN

A MANUAL FOR WORKING WITH
MIND, EMOTION, AND INTERNAL ENERGY

SERGE AUGIER

With translations by ISIS AUGIER
Foreword by DR. YANG, JWING-MING

SINGING
DRAGON
LONDON AND PHILADELPHIA

First published in 2015
by Singing Dragon
an imprint of Jessica Kingsley Publishers
73 Collier Street
London N1 9BE, UK
and
400 Market Street, Suite 400
Philadelphia, PA 19106, USA

www.singingdragon.com

Front cover image: painting by Isis Augier

Library of Congress Cataloging in Publication Data
Augier, Serge.
  Shen Gong and Nei Dan in Da Xuan : a manual for working with mind, emotion, and internal energy /
Serge Augier ; with translations by Isis Augier.
     pages cm
  ISBN 978-1-84819-260-7 (alk. paper)
  1. Taoist meditations. 2. Meditation--Taoism. I. Title.
  BL1942.8.A84 2015
  299.5'14435--dc23
                          2014036289

British Library Cataloguing in Publication Data
A CIP catalogue record for this book is available from the British Library

ISBN 978 1 84819 260 7
eISBN 978 0 85701 208 1

Printed and bound in Great Britain

To my wife Isis, my true love

Do not be fooled by nebulous, complicated writings.

*It should be simple, because this practice has
been developed by very practical people.*

It should be usable and easy to understand.

*You will discover through this tradition, as it is presented
here, the infinite possibilities that are within your reach.*

Contents

Part Seven: Wai Gong (Theory and Exercises for Training the Body)

Part Eight: Some Final Words

Foreword

I have known Serge for so many years now that I can't believe just how long it has been. When I met him for the first time at one of my seminars in London, he was maybe only 16 or 17 years old and I was in my 40s. He struck me as an enthusiastic young man filled with many dreams and a delightfully happy attitude towards life. I found him to be very humble and eager to learn, even though he already had great abilities. For many years after, he continued exchanging with me every time I traveled to Europe. Since then, we have built a lifelong friendship. Whenever I am in France, I always look forward to meeting with him and his family.

I am very pleased to see the progress that Serge has made over his many years of study, practice, research, and travel. In the time I have known him, I believe he has always continued to gain a deeper, more insightful understanding of health and life, year by year. He has traveled to China, Hong Kong, Japan, and other locations around the world to study Qigong, massage, and healing. I am happy to see how open-minded he is about both learning and sharing his knowledge. It is invaluable that such knowledge is constantly taught and made available to the world, such that all people can learn, improve, and enjoy a higher quality of life together.

I still remember Serge as an ambitious young visionary. Today he has succeeded in making his dreams come true. Through persistence, patience, and humility, he has set a very good example for the new generation to follow. A disciplined mind can accomplish anything. His work and influence will surely help pioneer a stronger and more promising future for the development of healthy, well-balanced living. Traditional Chinese medicine and complementary medicine are still not as widely accepted by the Western world as I have been hoping. We need more pioneers to plant seeds, to enable people to heighten their own self-awareness and capabilities. I sincerely believe that if all of us join in sharing what we have learned about life, together we will undoubtedly bring the world to a higher level of peace and harmony.

I sincerely wish Serge all the very best for his new and continued dreams, as he continues to write, publish, teach, and travel.

Dr. Yang, Jwing-Ming
Director, YMAA California Retreat Center
November 27, 2014

Part One

Basic Principles and Theory

The Mountain Practice and the Five Arts

In our tradition—Da Xuan, or the Big Secret—we talk about the Five Arts that make our system complete: Mountain, Destiny, Divination, Medicine, and Observation.

As students of the Way, we mainly focus on one of them—the practice (the "Mountain")—and it is on this aspect that this book concentrates. It is helpful to understand all five arts to see the full picture, and in future volumes of this series we will explain the theories and practices relating to the other four. In this book, however, we focus on the first aspect and particularly on the training of the mind, ego, energy, and emotions.

In China, when the system was developed, students were given key words because this was an oral tradition in which everything was learned by heart. Around the key words there were many long stories. Each story had a key word and the key word enabled the students to remember all the detail of the long story.

Mountain

The mountain is the symbol of personal cultivation. When you train, you "go to the mountain." Typically, however, our tradition is in the world; you do not retire into the mountains. You have a family and a job. So even though you go to the mountain when you train, you stay in the city. We are not a tradition of retirement from the world.

Going to the mountain is more a symbol, comprising the five aspects of practice:

- Wai Gong (external training)

- Nei Gong (internal training)

- Nei Dan (inner alchemy)

- Shen Gong (mind training)

- Xin Yi Dao Yin Fa (emotion training).

The five aspects are aspects of the interaction of the Three Treasures (mind, body, and energy). When you train the body (Wai Gong) and then train the breathing (Nei Dan), you come to realize that there is a missing link. When you train the body, the mind focuses on the exercise to correct the motion. When you start the breathing exercises by sitting still, the body does not necessarily adapt. It can be painful and the first reflex is the desire to move. Training the body is called external training.

The link between external training and breathing is called internal training (Nei Gong).

Internal training can be explained as follows. When you have trained physically for some time, you know the motion well and do not need to think about it. The mind is then free to focus on the sensation during the motion. This is when you switch from external training, Wai Gong, to internal training, Nei Gong. The training follows the same movements but the intent is different. Your mind switches focus from correcting the motion, or even remembering the motion, to paying attention to the breathing. Then when you sit down for the breathing exercises, Nei Dan, your mind knows how to hold the body. So in fact from the two treasures—body and energy—you have three aspects of training:

Wai Gong (external exercises), Nei Gong (internal exercises), and Nei Dan (inner alchemy, breathing).

The link between the body/energy and the mind is the emotional training.

We still have to work on mind training. Shen Gong is just the meditative aspect; as soon as you want to switch from breathing training to mind training, you will have a problem. Because of all the energy you have acquired, emotions arise when you start to put all your intention on your mind.

Emotions will be bothersome mainly because you are not familiar with them. They look like enemies but it also feels strange if you do not have them.

To deal with this aspect and improve our relationship with our emotions, we have a special training called Xin Yi Dao Yin Fa—the training of emotions. Then, finally, we have pure mind training— Shen Gong. I won't use the term "meditation" because that means everything and nothing nowadays. Shen Gong is simply training of the mind. The mind becomes your tool, and you are no longer the tool of your mind.

This is a very brief introduction to the five aspects of the practice that we need to train in order to have a complete practice of the Mountain aspect.

Chapter 1

Fundamental Principles

The Three Treasures: San Bao

A very important aspect of this tradition is San Bao, which translates as "the Three Treasures." These are vitality (Qi), mind (Shen), and body (Jing). We have to understand that these three aspects are actually at the same level. One is no more important than the other. This means that we have to train the three aspects all the time. If we don't, we get stuck in one of the aspects. For a long time it will be necessary to train these aspects separately. Consider a mixed salad. You might think that because there are a lot of ingredients you can just throw in anything; on the contrary, in order for all the flavors to combine perfectly, every ingredient should be of the best quality.

The same is true in your training. You have to train the body. Then you have to train the energy (breathing exercises) and then you have to train the mind. The difference between the mind and the breathing is that in the breathing you actually focus on something physical that exists. In the training of the mind (Shen Gong), you train something that does not exist. If you feel it, it has become materialized in the body—through emotion, for instance—and it is no longer the training of the mind. We have to make sure we are able to differentiate each aspect and then everything develops well. Then you can mix all aspects without getting confused.

Usually, I avoid using the Chinese characters because it creates a sort of mystery that we really do not need when trying to be clear about what we are doing. However, it is interesting to examine the Chinese characters for these Three Treasures.

Qi 氣

The main significance here is energy. A lot of people see Qi as something very mysterious, but the character is simply air on the top and grain, or rice, on the bottom. Qi is what you breathe and what you eat. Training the Qi involves physical exercises that will help your breathing and eating. The Qi you acquire comes from the food you eat and from your breathing. If you want more energy, then breathe better and eat better!

Shen 神

Shen is the mind and its character is also very interesting. On the left side there is an altar with smoke going to the gods; the other part of the character illustrates thunder going from heaven to earth. This indicates that our Shen is our connection with something higher. Whether we believe it or not does not matter. We know our mind has no limit and has infinite possibilities—the highest possibilities of the human being. Sometimes you get a sense of things you should or should not do that arrives out of nowhere; if you follow this guidance, it usually works. This is your connection to the higher. Shen is the part of a human being closest to absolute Yang and heaven; if you are relaxed enough, it will make your intuition better.

Jing 精

Also called essence, Jing is the body. Its character is represented by the same plant, the grain of rice, that is represented in the Qi character. This means that the first basic energy given to you without doing anything is Jing. In the body, the essence you already have is the will to be alive. But the second part of the plant is the hidden root. This means that Jing is a potential, which has everything inside but has not yet been revealed. You just need to go and look for it to live it fully. If you do not go and look for it, the plant will still grow, but you will not be living to your maximum potential.

The Celestial Mandate, the Chinese Daoist astrology, gives you all the elements of your life, but in fact everything you are supposed to do in your life is contained in Jing, which carries all the information—just like a grain contains all the information to become a plant. Jing is very similar to DNA in that we have all the information in Jing. To realize it completely, however, we need to see it. It is not that it is hidden, but it is in the dark. In fact, the name of our tradition, Da Xuan, means the Great Secret. It does not imply that we are hiding something, but simply that it is in the dark and that we need to cast light on it. It is the same with Jing. It is hidden, but if you train long enough, you realize what you have to do to fulfill your potential. Also, Jing is the body, the container in which you will put all the good elements. If the container is weak, you cannot use it. Furthermore, the training consists in many things, and if the training is to last a long time, then this implies that you have to stay healthy a long time, thus having a strong body. Otherwise, you cannot train.

Innate and acquired Jing

You have two types of Jing. One is energy given by your Jing, your essence that was there when you were created as a human being. The essence of your father and mother meet; when it works, the Yuan Shen (spirit) makes a spark. The two Jings create a third Jing in which you already have energy, the desire to live, and what was given by your parents (good or bad). This is innate Jing that exists before you are born. There is nothing you can do about it. Then you have post-heaven Jing, which is energy that you acquire and that you can build. Let's say your parents gave you very poor Jing, which means your countdown to death is very short. Each time you are tired in the day means your acquired Jing has been used up. If you carry on with your activities even though you feel tired, you will be using the innate Jing and you will make your little counter go faster. This will clearly show: you will grow older faster.

What you have to do is build up abundant acquired Qi through training so that you never have to use the innate Qi. Say you just have two dollars in the bank (poor Jing) but you never spend it because people offer you enough to live on; you don't need to worry that your innate Jing is good or bad because there are ways to protect it and never use it. This is the training.

Principles for practice 1

It is necessary to understand the Yin–Yang concept in order to understand not only which training but also what types of food and lifestyle are good for you.

When you start training, first you need the basics. With your teacher or instructor, you receive information and you just have to follow what is said. Then, by training, the teaching seeps into you a little and it gives you enthusiasm. If you do not find this enthusiasm and still have to force yourself to train after years of practice, then there is a problem. Indeed, the teaching, which is Yang, comes into you by practicing, which is Yin. So the teaching that you make your own brings out the Yang—Fire, and thus joy and happiness. Then it becomes necessary to find the right balance between Yin and Yang. If you do too much, you burn out quickly; if you do too little, nothing works.

We compare training to cooking: it is the "fire regime." There is only one thing we know for sure with the training. It is like making water boil. How long the water will take to boil depends on how much fire you have under the pan, but the water *will* eventually boil. However, if you keep taking the pan of water off of the burner before it boils, it will never boil. This means that even if you train a little, that's OK, but you need to train every day. There is no weekend or Sunday off when it comes to training!

Training is a way to be. The only thing we know is that we have to train all the time and then the water boils. The problem is knowing how much fire we need.

In the evolution of the practice, as a new student, you go from getting the information, training with the information, getting the knowledge to become yourself, to finding enthusiasm and using it to really train and then regulate the training. After a while, training too much can be as bad as not training enough, because at some point you will just burn out. Some people need to reach this point to find their balance, but it is better not to go too far because it can take a very long time to recover. You may even get tendon problems and inflammation because your structure (Yin) cannot stand the motion (Yang), especially when you are undertaking martial arts training with weapons. Too much Yang will cause inflammation. On the other hand, if you do not do enough, your body will become flabby with an accumulation of Yin—fat. If you are too Yin, you can no longer ignite the Yang.

Principles for practice 2

Let's look at how the Yin–Yang principle is applied to training the body. The Yin–Yang concept can explain everything, including the way we train.

If you train and you stop, you realize that you have a lot of energy, but the energy goes away. This is because when you train, you have a tendency to create Yang energy, and Yang energy rises. You will feel warm—you can even warm up the room. But you want to keep this energy and not just be a heater for the room!

If you go back to Yin–Yang theory, it gives you the answer on how to train. Yang is more action than Yin, but Yang is also subtler than Yin. It can be the mind. If I decide to build a table, preparing myself to build it is Yin and building the table is Yang. But we might also say that the thinking—planning the construction—is Yang, and materializing of the plan by building it is Yin.

So how do I train for the Yang energy to stay in my body? Action is Yang, and the body—the structure—is Yin. I want to transform my body structure with Yang because I cannot transform with Yin. You need Yang action to transform Yin structure. You cannot just stand immobile, stare at yourself in your mirror, and develop your body. If you take a weight and start lifting it with your arms, using your biceps muscles, the Yang action will make the Yin structure move.

If you do it for a little while, your arm will become warmer. But that doesn't change the structure. If you continue your exercise long enough with the correct intensity, however, Yang motion will change Yin structure. You gain muscle mass as the Yin, transformed by the Yang, becomes better Yin. This improved Yin can do more Yang motions, which will keep developing the Yin until it reaches the best it can be (which is your Jing—the hidden root). There will come a point at which your Yang and your Yin are at their best and you are at the maximum of your ability. Then you can move on to the next stage.

Key words for the path of training

Every aspect of the practice has key words so that you can remember what you must look for when you train. The key words, whether for internal or external training, are the qualities developed in each aspect of the training. As soon as you start the practice, you want to develop qualities that you will keep training throughout your practice.

1. Feeling

You need to learn how to feel. This means not only feeling your body in space but feeling the warmth of your hand in contact with the cold air, feeling the difference between your muscles, tendons, and bones, feeling the air exchange in your body, and so on.

It goes from very simple things such as feeling your body in motion, in space, to more subtle aspects such as the feeling around your hand depending on where it is in space, or feeling the difference between training alone or training with people next to you. There is a difference, for instance, between the sensation when your hand is a few inches from your thigh and a few inches from the ground. If you train long enough, your sensations become more acute. You need to feel as much as you can during the day and whenever you train.

This is also very useful when you practice traditional Chinese medicine, Daoist medicine, and martial arts.

2. Linking

Your body needs to be linked as one. This means that if you move your arm, the movement is in fact coming from your back, your hips, your legs, and your feet on the ground. Even if you are sitting down, the motion has to be linked. Your body should not move as if each part is separate. The whole body has to participate as one in every movement. This is how we save energy.

3. Grounding

You need to be grounded in order to keep your energy. If your Yin structure is weak and not grounded, the Yang energy generated from the exercises will just disappear. In order to keep the energy, you have to store it. This is the concept of inner alchemy. It has to stay inside. For this we need grounding. Every motion has a direction and a relationship to the earth you are standing on. Feeling, linking, and grounding are the three qualities we need to train for external and internal training.

Principles for practice 3

When you feel tingling or warmth, cold pain, or swelling in your hand or body, it is *not* energy. It is the energy trying to flow into something that is completely blocked. Later, when you get the feeling of energy, it is something very smooth and not manifested.

It is just like the electric current in a cable. It is not the electricity that creates the heat but the friction of the current trying to force its way into something that is resisting it.

Three aspects of physical training
1. Strengthening

One thing that will come by itself when you train every day is strength. You will never look like a bodybuilder, but you will become stronger because you are using your body as a whole. Everything you do seems easier because you are more aligned and coordinated. In fact, you are using your body more wisely.

When you are stressed, your body is tense and uses more strength than is necessary in little daily motions. You can imagine the energy wasted for this. An experiment measured the force used by the most stressed university student while eating soup. It was found that he was using the equivalent of 7kg of force to bring his spoon of soup up to his mouth!

If you use your body as a whole for all your daily actions, you will not be wasting energy. This is why you feel more vitality and strength. You are not yet *gaining* energy, however. This will happen after some time when your continuous Yang training changes your Yin structure. Then you will actually be getting stronger.

Another aspect of strength is the abundance of Qi acquired. This "excess" of vitality is very beneficial in order to stay healthy. However, it may change the way your body reacts to illness. When your energy level is high, each time you get sick the symptoms will be more intense. These symptoms show that your body is defending itself!

When they start training, many people complain, "I was never sick before; how can I get sick now that I am doing something good for my body?" In fact, before they began training, their defensive energy was not strong enough to fight, so the illness would gradually seep in deeper and deeper. When your Qi is empty, you don't fight, but the illness makes you function on a lower level and gradually brings you down. You don't feel it, but it becomes deeper and worse. In contrast, with excess Qi, as with children, the slightest cold will bring high fever. You no longer have this gradually increasing deficiency when you train; each time there is a problem, your body fights to get back to zero.

Being strong also means that this abundance of Qi will solve other daily problems: you will not feel tired, you will sleep better, and your digestion will be more efficient.

According to the Chinese Daoist concept, it is not the muscles that give force; they are only the vector for tendons. The actual use of force comes from the tendons, which is why, in our tradition, we train them through twisting and turning in our motions. This is what develops the specific strength in our system.

2. Relaxing

Becoming loose and relaxed means the body is able to function as a whole and move without tension. This implies coordination. If you see someone doing a movement that does not challenge your normal ability (as opposed to a gymnast doing backflips!), you should be able to watch and reproduce the movement. It should not be difficult for your body to reproduce something you understand and that is within your reach physically. If after trying for an hour you still cannot reproduce the motion, however, this means that you have a problem of proprioception and coordination. These two qualities are directly linked to the fact of being really relaxed or not.

Normally, if your mind understands and your body works, together they should be able to reproduce the motion. There are many of these plans of motion that are not connected properly between the mind and body. This is the first hurdle, when people realize their lack of coordination. This is when some people leave the practice!

Being relaxed is what keeps you healthy. When you are clear as to what comes from your mind, what comes from your body, and the connection between the two, everything goes more smoothly.

3. Grounding

Being physically grounded means that if someone pushes you or pulls you, you stay there. This is something we train a lot. And, in fact, this training does not remain something purely physical.

If you are really grounded, you realize that this also applies to your mind and emotions. This is very important because when we train we experience a great deal of emotional challenge; if you have a lot of grounding, it helps. As soon as you start energetic work you can quickly lose track of reality and become a bit disconnected. Grounding is crucial for this as it creates the necessary balance for the spiritual work. Otherwise, it can really go wrong! It is not good to be too mundane, but it is even worse to be too disconnected.

In our system, we need to defend and occupy our space. We have to be there. And to be there we must be grounded. This is also very important for martial arts.

The static postures are a good way of training how to align and ground the body. We start by standing, but it can also be done sitting or lying down. All the static training, however, is best done standing up; it will more easily create Qi and give you grounding. You generate Yang energy very readily with the static positions and this Yang energy will be felt easily because you are not using it for motion. If you keep a slight tension in your fingers and your arms open, this will also train the tendons in a specific way. It also makes the fascia develop in specific ways to protect the cavities of the body. The Yang energy transforms the Yin structure and makes the body fuller. It is a way to quieten not only the noises in your head but also any kind of tension in the body. Then you start to be aligned and everything is possible.

Part Two

Introduction to Shen Gong
(Mind Training)

Chapter 2

Important Principles

In our school, the basis of our practice is represented with an image of Man between Sky and Earth, which is also the basis of ancient clan Daoism. This image is extremely important as it reminds us of our balance and our place in the universe.

According to this representation, we must:

1. recognize our instinctive and animal aspects, our body, and love all these aspects equally

2. recognize equally our infinite aspect with no limits

3. recognize that we are torn between these two sides, Sky and Earth, with an energetic perception of things. This energetic perception is typically a trait of humans (as opposed to plants and animals).

It is the perfect balance of these three elements on the same level that makes a difference to us as a human being. This is the balance that the student of the Way will be trying to achieve through the practice. In line with this, Shen Gong training offers the possibility to live happily in society with our family and work, but also to be able to live the other aspects of our human nature by developing our spirituality and transforming our destiny.

Why train the mind?

The main reason to work on the mind is to perfect it. There is always the idea of improving it. But how can you improve, develop, and transform something you do not know? The main problem is that we do not know how we work internally. We do not know what and why we change, why some emotions and thoughts arise from nowhere; why, sometimes, memories come up while we are doing something completely different. We do not understand the mind's processes.

So before we can even begin to work on the mind, we must first learn to know it better.

The training to do with learning how the inner mind works is often put aside and neglected by the student because it is the hardest part of the training.

The spiritual, meditative, or even religious work in all traditions involves the undoing of the mind's processes in order to go back to the beginning. At first we are united with nothingness; we then dissociate to become a particular being. The purpose is to return to something united. In order to achieve this, or at least part of it, we must deconstruct what the mind has developed. But the mind will do everything to keep its individuality and will develop defense mechanisms accordingly.

> *Dissociating the mind means no longer existing the way the mind has established itself, and this implies dying. This is what we fear most and this is why the mind defends itself in so many elaborate ways.*

As a child, this individuality is rather blurry, but it is developed by the mind and established firmly around adolescence. This is what will help to shape our personality, but it will go against who we really are naturally. Therefore, Shen Gong is a very important part of our practice because it is a way to clear the mind from what it has gradually built as a defense mechanism, and then balance it and let who we really are naturally arise.

Another reason, which must not be forgotten, is that mind training brings us the possibility to reach true happiness in life. This is possible when you achieve the first part of the practice.

A difficult endeavor

Trying to see how the mind works, even watching it like a spectator, puts the mind in danger. As we have seen above, dissociating the mind leads to its death. Shen Gong is clearly the gate to the acceptance of death. This is what makes it so difficult to train Shen Gong.

Also, it is a difficult task to train something non-manifested. Clearly the mind is non-material. Consequently, the student does not really know what to do: just sitting down and watching how your mind works is not very pleasant. Also, you do not feel you are improving in any way, which can be frustrating. Finally, and most importantly, it is very disappointing!

> Indeed, we all believe we are so great, profound, and interesting, but once we start watching our mind work in an unfocused way, we realize how messed up it is, how it will not stay still, and how it is out of control.

Furthermore, often what comes out is not great revelations but smaller insignificant subjects.

Unfortunately, we have to go through this stage since it is the most important part of any work on the mind. It is the true base for any possible work to develop, perfect, and transform the mind. These goals all require technique, and we will describe the methods further below.

Don't give up!

Even the very first stage of observing your mind requires some technique. When you sit down to watch your mind, you can very easily and quickly become wrapped up in a train of thought and end up spending two hours having done nothing else! In other words, there has not been one instant of silence and you may feel that you failed. In fact, this is not true!

> *The great and motivating aspect of Shen Gong is that no matter how badly you think you performed your exercise, you will still be improving your Shen Gong. The worst work will still be a success.*

The Shen Gong exercises work by accumulation. It is the repetition of sitting down every day and training that will make a difference and enable the mind to let go. Every minute spent training your Shen Gong will be cumulated and will be positive. Even if you spend the two hours of your exercise thinking how lousy you are and how useless it is, but still repeat this every day, it will be a success! Indeed, at some point you will move on to something else and another level. The only thing that can keep you from improving is to stop the training.

Imagine if the mind were someone important to you. You would want to spend as much time as possible with that person in order to get closer to them, to know and understand them better. Each minute together would be more fruitful than not seeing them. It is the same for the mind. It is always better to spend a little time observing the mind than saying that there is not enough time for it to be worth it.

Stages of evolution and moments of consciousness

Spending long periods of time on your Shen Gong will accelerate your evolution and you will be able to catch glimpses of things you normally could not witness when your mind is still a mess or at the beginning of the work. You might not be at a stage of evolution where you can attain these true experiences; however, you can live moments of consciousness at any time throughout your practice. Therefore, when you put yourself in specific states during long periods of practice, you can touch ultimate moments without being ready for this. This gives you a feeling of where you are heading.

This is the only advantage of long, directed practices. In no way, however, does this mean you have reached those stages of evolution where true experiences occur.

> *The only true evolution is through the repeated daily observation of the mind. This regular work is what brings you to stages of evolution.*

Stages of evolution are deeply connected to the way we operate. Thus, evolving happens according to our work, in contrast to moments of consciousness, which are not linked to our evolution. Indeed, these are triggered by a combination of elements, working in synergy, which will expose us to these moments.

It is the difference between moments of connection to the absolute, God or consciousness and moments of realization. It is not because you are looking through a window at something perfect, absolute, that you are perfect. You will not be transformed by this vision. You must work at your own evolution and realization. The slow, constant, and gradual work is what will bring you to stay in these evolved states. Once you have reached a level of evolution, you cannot regress. True evolution always goes in the same direction. For instance, once you learn how to speak and understand a language, you cannot keep yourself from understanding what is being said. It comes naturally and you cannot regress in your knowledge and understanding of the language. The same is true with swimming. Once you know how to swim, your body does not forget. If you fall into water, your body will naturally move in order to stay at the surface; you cannot unlearn this. Before, however, when you did not know how to swim, you could drown immediately. Once you have reached a specific stage of evolution, you have passed it and can no longer go back. Furthermore, you always evolve in the same direction.

Studies have shown that this is also true in the evolution of groups. We always evolve in the same direction and there is never a regression. In every ancient tradition there was an awareness of this evolution. This is why many traditions use techniques or/and drugs to live moments of consciousness during initiation rituals as this reveals the direction—an idea of where one will be heading through the rest of the practice. But these initiations, because of their specific purpose, usually only occur once in the early stages of the person's evolution.

How does the practice of Shen Gong evolve?
1. Mind out of control
At first, when you watch your mind, you will notice that your mind is out of control, with illogical trains of thought running through you and great agitation. If you repeat this exercise long enough and keep watching your mind, this constant agitation will be tainted with a certain flavor. This specific flavor is linked to your emotions.

2. Emotions
With this new element, you enter the second stage.

Emotions are present to protect the mind so that we never reach it.

Emotions enable us to live without the mind, as perceptions will go straight into the emotional level, and hence the body and its manifestations.

    a. The major emotion, connected to all others, is *fear*. We all have it and it is linked to the refusal to go back to what dissociates, because we would disappear. We all fear death and anything that reminds us of the fact we are going to die. But fear can be hidden. It is usually hidden by two other emotions:

b. *Sadness.* The idea of dying can make you sad. It is only once you have overcome this sadness, by accepting death as part of life, that your intimate fears will arise.

c. *Anger.* I am angry because I want to be immortal!

This trilogy of fear, sadness, and anger is the basis for how we operate. It often works in layers. For instance, you first feel sadness, which in fact conceals anger, which hides fear. Or you have anger hiding sadness hiding fear. After a while, when you have watched your mind even longer, you come to realize that these emotions are expressed through recurrent feelings: sadness expressed through resignation or boredom, anger through helplessness, or confusion through anxiety and fear. You are completely into the second stage at this point.

What is interesting in this process of watching the mind is that it started out with something unidentified which became something recognizable in its structure. Once you experience this and truly realize it, you move into the third stage.

> *Note: Being aware of this is not something you learn and know intellectually. The awareness must come directly from a clear experience during the exercise.*

3. Looking to see what's behind

The third stage, in the beginning, is when recurrent messages, traumas, and matters waiting to be resolved arise during Shen Gong.

> *Once again, the work on the mind starts with a big mess—the original chaos; then comes the filter from your emotions and you can see what is problematic.*

Here the problems are purely mental (they become emotional once you become aware of them). The original message, image, concept, or trauma deriving from the problem is a product of the mind; thus it does not exist. You just have perceptions of it. All of these elements are what create our personality with its dysfunctions, its defense mechanism, and how we operate in the world.

> Note: Our personality is not who we are. It comes from our "persona," the mask behind which we hide.

With this third stage, slowly and gradually you are evolving from the "one you think you are" to "the one you think you are, while looking to see what's behind."

Let's imagine a wall. In this stage you are just able to climb up the wall for a few seconds to catch a glimpse of something on the other side. However, it is too dark to really see; as in "Xuan," the mysterious, it is not hidden, but you cannot see it because it is too dark. You *do* know something is there, whereas before you had no clue!

The wall beforehand represented the end of the world. In fact, the wall is an emotional barrier and what is not understood. But you sense that behind the wall is some mystery. Here the term "Xuan," the mysterious, picks up the idea developed in our school, "Zin Ran," the natural, in that everything is perfect inside; you just need to let it out. This implies that the "mysterious" is not hidden or imperceptible; it is right there but in a place where there is not enough light to see it.

Therefore, we have to add more light in order to see it. The mind, directed in the right way, detached from the mental process and emotions, *is* light. By practicing your Shen Gong and following a course of action in your everyday life—being aware and correcting the way you behave and the way you judge things—the thick wall described above will gradually thin down to a veil.

The three stages above are what bring us to the real Shen Gong practice.

On all levels Shen Gong is the most therapeutic of all the practices.

> *Wai Gong (body work) will reinforce your body and correct your position and movements. Nei Dan (inner alchemy) will develop the breath and bring vitality. Shen Gong will reset your mind, cleaning it from traumas and rebalancing it. In that sense it is definitely therapeutic.*

We have a spiritual vision of the mind's evolution. We see Shen Gong as a way to find and catch the monsters and demons in our mind, transform them, and sublimate them. This is known as spiritual therapy, spiritual transformation, or "porosity to light." Many traditions have this similar vision of balancing the mind and perfecting it to get closer to God, to infinity. This also implies that devotion can be a tool but is not the end, since the goal is to fuse with infinity. You cannot unite if you remain victim to your mental mind. On the other hand, from a regular therapeutic standpoint, the work would simply help you to identify these demons and learn how to live with them.

How can the mind—the ego—trick you?

Once again, the mind always wants to defend and protect itself from any observation since this can bring about its dissolution. The mind will defend its individuality, the ego, mainly through commenting on and judging what you are doing during your practice. When your ego is very strong and feels it is not being heard, it can even send messages through the body to divert you from your practice—such as drowsiness, headaches, nausea, itchiness, or soreness. These manifestations tend to last only a short time. Once you know about these possible effects, you just let them happen and accept them, and they will eventually disappear. You know this is a trick and you just go along with it, knowing this will not affect your training.

If you are uncertain about the veracity of what you are feeling (Am I really hurting? Is this tingle in my toe real? Is my nose really itching like crazy?), dive into the feeling and just focus on it for a little while. If it is a trick, you will notice that the feeling can intensify for a brief moment and then it just disappears. This is because the truth dissolves what is false.

The ego can also trick you into feeling superior. Indeed, in order to get you to stop practicing, the mind will make you believe you do not need to train in order to evolve, that you are better than this. You find this problem in the idea of "material spirituality." Your mind will find ways to make you believe you have reached spirituality, that you are a spiritual being and needn't practice.

This is the reason that spiritual systems where visualization is the main technique will be much more successful in terms of numbers of followers. First and foremost, keep in mind that visualization is only mental. Since you are using your mind and imagination in order to complete the exercise, it will obviously be much more satisfying. Here the mind is used and the ego solicited; we do not watch it like a spectator.

The mind does not feel in danger and, worse, in these methods the ego is nicely polished and cultivated to the extreme!

Thoughts, images, colors, and comments
1. Thoughts

We have seen how thoughts work by branching out like a tree and can continue endlessly if there is no conscious attempt to tame the mind. As we will see later on, the mind cannot think of several things at once. Only one thought can appear at a time. The chaos is not a proliferation of different thoughts all at once. Instead, it caused by the fast movements from one thought to the other in all directions.

2. Images

Images are considered a subtler, more hidden form of thought. Images deliver a message without words. They are directly linked to our sight, which is the most mental of the five senses. Images often replace pure thoughts when the mind has slightly quietened down, having spent some time watching it.

3. Colors

The succession of colors is another manifestation of the mind, not as defined as the two above but often tainted with emotions. If you are able to remain free from comments during the observation of these colors, you will come to the stage where all the specific problems, messages, and traumas are revealed. This is also true with recurrent sounds (most people do not experience this, but it can be the case if your perception of sounds is more developed —if music is your profession, for instance).

4. Comments

Comments and judgments are not thoughts, images, or colors, so to speak. Comments come from the commentator or the critic. We define this as a little inner judge that always has the same type of reactions and comments to things, and almost has its own personality! Comments and judgments are dangerous for our practice as they can induce the production and multiplication of thoughts and distract you from the exercise even more than the object of observation itself. The inner critic cannot exist without thoughts! When the commentator calms down, thoughts calm down, and when there are no more thoughts, the commentator disappears. In fact, there are several commentators connected to each facet of the mind.

There is your true nature, which you can access through meditation, but you need the person "who you think you are"— your ego—in order to function in the world.

What you don't need is the "one you claim to be."

Depending on the context (family or work) and the people you are interacting with, you can change your personality slightly. The main reason for this is to make sure people like you, and it is done more or less consciously. Each time you claim to be someone different, you will automatically add more commentators in your mind and it will end up being a big mess in your mind. Consequently, your choices in life are not in tune with who you really are quieten, and you are bound to be unhappy.

Principles for practice

The training becomes a practice only when you are alone. When you are in the school as a group, you train together to correct and learn, but this is never your actual practice. Practice is only by yourself for yourself.

In our path there are two aspects that should be balanced. You have to correct yourself; you must always keep learning and evolving. On the other hand, in order to really be in the practice, you must let go of the corrections and just train.

If you don't let go of the corrections, even with a good heart and good intentions, you will not be truly practicing and you can stay the same for years with no true evolution. If you do not practice, you do not evolve.

Our goal is to gradually eliminate all the little critics from all the different facets of our personality and finally get to the main critic and make it quieten down. This implies no longer pretending, being as close to your true nature as possible through the "one you think you are," and acting the same way no matter what the context.

The three minds

Traditionally, there are three minds: the one you think you are, the one you really are, and the one you pretend to be.

First, there is the commentator. This is the ego, the voice we hear in our head that is who we think we are. In fact, this is not who we are. It is this "mental" mind that enables you to operate in daily life. But sometimes certain situations in life make you act in a surprising way. All of a sudden you do not recognize yourself any more. This often happens in emergency situations where you do not have time to think. This means there is something else behind the person you think you are! Furthermore, if you are commenting on something in your head, it means you must have something to comment on! This implies there is something behind the ego.

The second mind is who you really are. You can connect to this mind by training, but you do need your mental mind in your daily life. These two are pretty much who we are: something absolute and something practical.

But then there is a third one: the one you pretend to be. This mind is all the different personalities you develop depending on who you are interacting with. You probably have noticed that people do not behave the same way when they are with family, a partner, a friend, or work colleague. The more fake characters you have created, the more you will develop bad feelings about yourself and the more you will have emotions that come from nowhere.

This good news is we can get rid of the one we pretend to be! The more you behave and act the way you think you are, the better you feel. Then you will only have to face the real problems, the ones rooted deeply in who you are. There is less friction in your mind between all the different roles and suddenly your mind is much clearer. When you face your true problems, it is similar to what happens in dreams. Often you can experience your dreams in so many different ways, but you always have a few recurrent things expressed in different ways. These are the real issues.

The body and the practice of Shen Gong

As you know, in our practice there is a connection between the body, the breath, and the mind. Although the mind work does not necessarily require great vitality and physical health to evolve, it is important to recognize that the greater the vitality, the more you will be able to train the mind in the long run. We are not striving for reincarnation through a rapid cycle of life to move on to another life cycle, nor are we searching for a life of abandonment. We simply want to live in society, for the longest time possible and in the best way possible. Unlike the Indian traditions, for instance, where the body is controlled for a superior purpose (the mind), in our tradition we do not forget or compromise the body. Besides, practicing in the world, rather than living as a recluse, requires maintaining a balance between the body and the mind.

Indeed, the work on the mind is very Yang. It can cause very intense emotions to surface and can create a lot of inner agitation. If the body is not strong enough to ground you during the practice, it can create serious problems. Therefore, once again, the most important aspect is the balance between body, breath, and mind. Furthermore, if you trained the physical and breath aspect, you will be able to use the qualities developed (alignment, center, stillness, breathing) to make Shen Gong easier.

In order to practice Shen Gong, you must be:

1. Comfortable

If you are not comfortable, it will *not* work because your mind will focus on the discomfort. If you are in pain or ill, the same problem will arise since your focus will be altered.

2. Aligned and with good posture

If you are aligned, your capacity to hold yourself is greater; this will avoid developing drowsiness and soreness in your body. Furthermore, developing your physical and energetic center will help with centering the mind as well.

3. Still

Stillness is very important. In fact, it is better to be crooked and still than aligned in motion! At the beginning of your Shen Gong work, when you are new to the process, stillness will help your concentration even if it is quite artificial. This implies complete immobility. You must force yourself to stay completely still, letting nothing go. This also implies making no noise and even breathing silently. It will be much easier to keep a regular breathing cycle if you have trained your Nei Dan first (work on breath). Proper breathing will bring better oxygenation and a feeling of wellbeing and joy, with a calming effect, which is very valuable during your Shen Gong.

Chapter 3

Exercises

How to begin

We begin Shen Gong training by developing two major ideas, which are:

1. getting to know your mind and

2. letting the natural come out.

The first two methods that follow enable us to develop in practice the two ideas above.

Exercise 1: Watching the mind

The first exercise is an introduction to Shen Gong.

Sit down and simply watch what is going on in your mind, intervening as little as possible. This means your mind will wander and keep giving more or less emotionally tainted information. However, you must not follow these pieces of information and you should not develop any comment on the given message/ thought. The comments are purely a product of the mind and are manifested through emotions. If you comment on your thoughts, this will maintain what your mind is used to doing—that is, branching out like a tree from one thought into endless thoughts.

You need to pull the plug in order to stop that cycle. The first way to start this process of silence is to stop commenting.

If you just follow your thoughts without intervention, you will notice that, instead of developing into a tree-like branching of thoughts, they will appear, rise, and fall much faster. If you are able to do this, you will then observe another rising thought and so forth. This way of watching your succession of thoughts, one by one, will gradually calm the mental chaos. This is something that evolves in the long run and is the most difficult aspect of our practice. Indeed, the physical aspect is much easier since your teacher can correct you all the time. He sees your mistakes and, even if he has to repeat things over and over, you will eventually succeed in reproducing the correct movement. The work on breath, Nei Dan, might seem more complicated; nevertheless, you can still follow specific instructions concerning your position and the way you use your diaphragm and abdominal muscles in order to keep the sensation, which will eventually pay off and give results.

But there is no way to correct, hold, and control the mind! Furthermore, the difficult thing about the mind is that if you push it too hard on one side, it will backfire and come back at you even harder from the other side! For instance, try telling yourself, "No matter what, at this moment I do not want to think of the color red." As a result you will only see red and think red, and it will be worse! The mind is like a little wild animal: you can try to tame it, but if you try to control it, it will just do the opposite of what you want it to.

The ability to remain neutral and uninvolved while watching your mind is what starts taming the mind. Like any basic skill, this capacity has to be developed by repeating the process. This means sitting down and watching your thoughts daily.

At the very beginning the thoughts are so chaotic that it makes it difficult to see one clear thought at a time. But this will come gradually. You will start to see one thought detaching from the existing mess. This is the thought you must observe, without comment. The emotional message will only rise after practicing this technique daily for some time.

Here we have seen how the first technique of Shen Gong consists in watching the mind, not in a quest for information but in order to reveal our deeper, natural way of operating. Once again, our true nature is hidden. We rarely know why we react the way we do. This technique is useful to become intimate with our mind and its ways, to understand our reactions, in order to know who we really are. This implies letting go of the person we think we are and gradually becoming our deeper hidden self. From this point on we can claim that we are working on transformation. It would be impossible to attempt transforming something you do not know. This is why we have to go through this process of watching the mind.

Exercise 2: The "yes" method

This method is a way to develop the concept of the natural. The natural is what is perfect inside, and this is what we are going to let out.

> *The training does not consist in adding elements to become natural but, on the contrary, in removing them: we remove our blocks, our defense mechanisms, and much more in order to let the natural express itself.*

You might think that our true nature would be educated through training but this is not exactly true. What is natural *is* natural and must be left this way since it is perfect the way it is. What must be trained are the behaviours and reactions in order to eliminate our blocks and enable the natural to reveal itself.

Shen Gong training is about letting go and removing, not adding. This idea is the basis of our second major method of Shen Gong: the "yes" method.

Since you are perfection deep inside, nothing should be rejected. This is a technique based on acceptance and non-resistance; it is the idea of going with whatever happens in your mind. Following the idea of non-resistance, you accept the products of your mind, your thoughts, comments, and emotions, without, however, investing yourself in them. So you just say "yes." This is a way of accepting and going with the flow of your mind. As soon as a new thought arises, you must consider it true and perfect, and love it as if it were the best thought ever! Do this without comment, of course. Here the "yes" is not a comment from the mind; it is an artificial intervention tainted with the emotions, with the feeling of love.

To reinforce the acceptance, you can smile slightly during the exercise. This is the faint smile you may notice on the statues of meditating Buddha. This changes everything about the way you apprehend your thoughts. During the practice of Shen Gong, when a thought arises, you watch it rise and develop, free of comment. In fact, simply the fact of observing a thought, even in silence, implies some kind of judgment. This judgment will be food for the thought and, by strengthening it, you cause the thought to grow and possibly branch out.

> *On the other hand, if you just accept and say "yes" to the developing thought, you will prevent it from growing, and the thought will actually fade away, lacking the nourishment it needs to develop. The "yes" removes the strength and dissolves the thought.*

Paradoxically, in this exercise you are hunting down your thoughts, even if you are seeking to accept and love them. The mind starts selecting thoughts carefully, and this is why they become more and more scarce.

This seems like a very straightforward and easy technique, but in fact it is very difficult in practice. Indeed, if all our thoughts were positive or self-glorifying, it might be easy to accept them with a "yes." But often this is not the case. One of the first defense mechanisms is our strategy to fail. The syndrome of failure is clearly a human trait. Therefore, the thoughts, emotions, and comments that will arise during this practice will often be negative.

Using the "yes" method therefore implies accepting everything that appears, even what you do not like. Saying "yes" to everything—good and bad—implies that whatever your mind presents as a message does not really matter, mainly because it could come up with the exact opposite thought just a few seconds later. These are all just moments. Since they are temporary, they can change from one instant to the next, which makes them unimportant.

> *The message itself, no matter how it is expressed, is never important. What is important is what it is pointing at.*

For instance, you feel weak. The message can be tainted with fear as this draws you back to your weakness. On the other hand, the message can express your importance and how you should be respected because this too is connected to how you feel about yourself—in this case, weak.

It is one of our reflexes to feel the need to express the reason why we do or do not agree with an idea. Here it is very hard to simply say "yes" with no argument or comment. Nevertheless, you may find it easier to practice this method at the beginning when your mind is still a mess. It is easier to say "yes" to a profusion of random thoughts than it is to a rising emotion. Then you usually want some real explanation and answer. Just having to accept an emotion as being perfect is very hard. Once you are able to repeat the exercise at a stage where emotions are coming out, you will notice that you feel lighter after each practice. In many traditions it is said that once you have accepted the world as it is you will levitate! Here the idea is the same. When you let go of things, you become much lighter.

The "yes" method is a very good way of calming the mind and making clearer what it needs to express. Moreover, you can experience moments of silence, pauses between thoughts, faster than with other techniques of Shen Gong because this method exhausts the mental process. For this reason it can be very satisfying.

Another aspect is that once the mind has quietened down sufficiently, the real problems, traumas, and shadows come out. During your practice, you can experience these real problems through thoughts or feelings, but at some point they will be very concrete, and once you finish your practice you will be able to identify and analyze these clearly. Sometimes you may not be certain about what is going on, but you may suddenly notice similar and specific behaviours from people around you. This is most likely a clear projection of your own problem, which you are trying to identify. Sometimes you can also find the answers in your dreams; during sleep you digest your daily emotions, including those experienced during your practice.

> *Note: Once you have identified your deep problems and shadows, the work will be focused on overcoming them but not fighting them. Indeed, since you are a perfect being, these problems and traumas are what helped shaped who you are and they will not disappear. With a specific strategy in Shen Gong we can overcome these negative aspects by neutralizing their trigger mechanisms. Once again, we cannot dissolve our shadows but we can bring light upon them. The shadows do not disappear but they no longer affect you because you have eliminated their manifestation. Despite its artificial aspect (saying "yes" to everything, including what you do not necessarily believe), this method, if repeated, will gradually free your mind.*

This technique can also be exported into your daily life! In many ways, saying "yes" to most things makes your life much easier. It enables you to let go and avoid being confrontational about everything. Paradoxically, it is also a very good tool for confrontation—saying "yes" dissolves aggression rather than feeding it.

Combined practice
Exercise 3: Observing attentively

This exercise is a way to combine the essence of "watching the mind" and the "yes" method. During this practice you put your full attention on each rising thought but do not comment in any way. You just wait to see what arises.

The main aspects of these three methods are as follows:

- In the first method you watch whatever comes up; you are not waiting for thoughts and you do not prepare anything. Depending on the type of thoughts that arise, you will simply observe them without interfering or commenting on them. In this method some thoughts may arise or there may also be nothing.

- In the second practice, the "yes" method, you will be attentive to what is arising in order to judge it in a positive way.

- In this third method you remain attentive but you do not judge what is happening. In that sense, it is a mix of the first two techniques.

These methods are the foundations of Shen Gong. They will help you know your mind better in order to act on it.

If you do not know yourself, you cannot change your behaviors and relationship to the world.

Chapter 4

Achieving Happiness by Calming the Mind

This is the aspect of Shen Gong accessible to people practicing in daily life and the most interesting part for us to study. This is the aspect in which we can develop happiness, nourished by inner peace. Our mind becomes our tool again, rather than the other way round. When the mind is calm, thoughts begin and end, instead of lingering on endlessly. Emotions do not arise as easily, so we simply feel good.

This aspect comprises 18 smaller parts, but essentially we are looking for three things.

1. Calming the mind by knowing the mind

First, we need to make the mind ours again. This means that it stops spinning on its own and stops commenting on everything. You cannot help or repair something if you do not know how it works.

Calming the mind is the aspect that you will find in most meditation manuals. Calming and soothing the mind means essentially knowing the mind. We want to know how the mind works in general, but particularly how our own mind works. We each have a way of functioning, which was determined by the age of three. Our perceptions will be interpreted and judged, qualified and organized. This will determine the way we think. This specific way of thinking will evolve with developed vocabulary and knowledge and imagination, but it will pretty much remain the same as far as the process itself is concerned. And this process is what differs from one person to another.

> *If you do not know the way you operate, there is no way you can correct it.*

This forms the first part of Shen Gong, with the idea of coming back to an available mind by calming it.

2. Occupying the mind

The second step is occupying the mind. Once you see how your mind works and you become more intimate with its process, you can start to occupy it. This means keeping it busy with exercises that will dissolve a big portion of the useless stuff in the mind. Indeed, our mind is constantly preoccupied by things that it should not be! Here we just need to give the mind some basic exercises (counting, working on the senses, etc.) that have the sole purpose of occupying it, so that eventually only the important things will remain. By doing this we go even deeper into our self-knowledge. We have calmed our mind, and now by occupying it we access information that we could not access before. When applied to the mind, these techniques enable the relevant information—the real issues—to reveal themselves. They also allow the mind to focus without forcing it to resolve problems. Indeed, we are not ordering the mind to concentrate. We find tools to allow the mind to do that on its own. If you order a child who is acting up and throwing a tantrum to stop, it will not work, but if you distract the child with something he likes, the crisis ceases immediately! This is exactly how our mind works. If you try to stop it, the mind will backfire and make it even worse.

3. Being focused

The third step is focusing. Imagine how much time you would save if your mind could really focus! Your relationships with other people will be much better because you will be 100 percent with them. You can work faster and you sense things more accurately. Everything benefits from being able to be focused.

There are three levels of focusing.

The first is concentration

Concentration is a closed-down vision—as in a reverse cone. This is not really a fun process. You just stare at something, concentrating for a certain amount of time. It is the most unfulfilling and "dumb" aspect of the training: just being able to be there, without thinking, and look at an object. Nevertheless, we really need this to improve our concentration. Especially today, when our lives do not depend on our ability to concentrate. We are no longer in survival mode, so we let go of this ability.

What does being concentrated mean? It means being able to stay concentrated consciously and willingly on the same object without being distracted from it for at least 30 minutes. This may seem very easy, but once you actually try you realize how difficult this is.

Concentration means that you are so completely focused on one point that the rest of the universe no longer exists. The only thing that exists is the object you are concentrating on. This creates a lot of tension and consumes a lot of energy, but it is necessary to go through this educational process in order to practice experiences.

The second is focusing

Focused attention is tunnel vision—when you are surprised by something that falls, for example, or are in a confrontation. When you are in a stressful or violent situation, you only see the person in question and the rest is a blur.

The third is attention

This is a relaxed focus. It is an open-cone vision. Instead of shutting down from the rest of the world to a specific point, here you go from you being the point outwards into the world. Attention means being conscious as much as possible of yourself and everything in your environment.

These three steps are the most important aspects of Shen Gong because they can lead you to happiness—the joy that comes from inside.

> *Remember that all perceptions come from the inside. There are never external perceptions.*

If your mind is in a balanced, happy state, then everything you perceive is positive. It is the same when you hear great news and the rest of the day is shaped by your good mood. This is really what we are looking for, but in a constant way.

Calming the mind exercises

There are many steps in this practice and most people stop after the first step, which is to look at your thoughts.

Exercise 1: Watching the mind

Calming the mind begins by looking at your mind. This consists of four stages: simple attention, observing and accepting your mind, active attention, and stillness.

The process of looking at your mind is the most tedious aspect of the practice and requires some endurance. It is as if you have a 100-yard race to run in a car that doesn't work. The hardest part is starting the car. This corresponds to watching your mind. Most people will stop trying before they get the car started, even though what follows is more easily within their reach.

Starting the car may take a while, but once you have started it, the rest is quite simple. When you understand your mind, you see more clearly the work needed. But most people get irritated and give up at this first step.

Simple attention

Simple attention means looking at your thoughts. This requires nothing. You sit down and close your eyes in order to have the least stimulation possible. And you look at what is going on in your mind. At first what you see will be a distorted vision of your own mind because it will rebel against the exercise, just as if you tell someone in an empty room to behave naturally while staring at them. The person will need some time to get used to your presence and to gradually let go of the pressure and relax. At some point they will even forget that you are watching them. So during these first encounters the mind will go through a lot of different phases before it can settle down again. It is usually during this chaotic or uninteresting period that people give up, because there is no valuable information, nothing stimulating to encourage them to continue. And also because we have preconceived ideas of what meditation should be like and grand ideas about what our mind is. It is quite disappointing!

In fact, this step is crucial and each moment you spend watching your mind adds to the other moments and will be important and beneficial for the rest of Shen Gong. Once again, the worst Shen Gong ever—that is, what you consider to be terrible—will still be good for your practice. You just have to keep at it and not give up. Of course, the time you spend doing this will affect your evolution. Spending all day practicing will obviously bring you to more advanced stages faster than 15 minutes a day. But you will eventually reach certain stages even with your daily 15 minutes! You need to be able to adjust the time according to your goals and then stick to it.

What happens at first?

1. When you first start watching your mind you will have to deal with non-stop commenting: your mind commenting on your thoughts and commenting on the fact that you are watching your mind commenting. This vicious cycle can be endless.

2. Then the mind rebels with the idea that what you are doing is a waste of time and you would be better off doing something else. Often what also comes up is that we are either too good or not good enough for this practice.

3. Once this calms down, it will be the thoughts about your day that will rise, such as your shopping list, the things you must not forget to do, and so on. This takes time! Even if this comes back constantly in your practice, you will notice that the moments when you are commenting on these daily thoughts will go by faster and you will instantly resume just watching your mind. Then more interesting elements start to appear.

4. Then at some point, just like hunters who have killed one or two ducks, there will be a moment when nothing happens. The other ducks stay still and silent for a moment. This deceiving tranquility will last for a while and then stronger elements will arise, often linked to current emotions.

   This tests the seriousness of your commitment to the tradition. Typically, these are moments when doubt will arise as your mind tries to find all the flaws in the system.

This is a difficult period because it is the commitment and true belief in the tradition that will become an anchor for you and help you to evolve through these steps. When you are clear about your choices, the mind will stop rebelling and will calm down, and this is when the more important information will come up. Often the emotions linked to the thoughts are not really identifiable and are not linked to something you are presently living. You could say they come out of the blue, and then the emotions are clarified. When an emotion arises, you know where it is coming from. However, there is no need for analysis; the understanding is natural. The fact of knowing its origin enables you to resolve it as well. Once again, this is a natural process that does not require an intellectual examination.

This first stage of watching the mind with simple attention can take quite some time—just like a pot over a fire. If you practice a bit, and then stop and start again, and then take another few days off, it will be like trying to make water boil by constantly taking the pot off of the burner. It will never boil. If you practice daily but for a short period, it will be like a low flame heating the water. It will also take some time to boil. You need continuity. Then real messages will arise from deep inside.

This leads us to the second step of watching your mind, which is to observe and accept your mind.

Observing and accepting the mind

This step can be done relatively quickly if you already have a practice in all aspects of the human being: body, mind, and vitality. Once what was deep inside of you emerges, you perceive much better the difference between who you are, who you pretend to be, and who you think you are. You are then able to have a lucid critical vision of your inner judge and commentator.

Once you are conscious of this inner jumble, you can accept it or not. As long as you do not accept who you are, including all these different facets, you will stay blocked in the same state. This is simply because you cannot be someone else and you will have to let go of prejudices, comparisons, expectations, fantasies about what you are, and your motivations.

Furthermore, your motivations—the reasons you come to meditate—are never good. Now that you are starting to know yourself better and you see this, you have to let it all go. If you are ready, this happens automatically—you just accept it naturally. Otherwise, it will still create tension and friction, and this can last a while.

This is a very Yin notion. We accept the concept of what we are through our incarnation. This is a difficult process because, all of a sudden, who you are—good and bad—becomes real.

What is interesting is that emotions are experienced through frustration and rising thoughts. Accepting who you are is not linked to emotions, however; when you experience an emotion, you are in confrontation with reality. On the contrary, in accepting who you are, you will feel soothed. This is the state in which the emotions also let go and you relax. This peacefulness is the feeling of neutrality in going back to the center.

Active attention

When you watch your mind with simple attention, a spontaneous emergence of thoughts comes to you. In active attention, we go from our deeper self towards our thoughts, and we await them. And then once we see them, we destroy them. This means watching the rising thought emerge and making it go away.

This is a simple mental process. Along with the rising thought comes a multitude of comments. You just have to stop this and return to the "white screen." This idea will be described below.

Exercise 2: Thought hunting

This "thought hunt" brings inner and outer tension, but it also triggers the thoughts to stop. Just as animals stay hidden when hunters are around, the thoughts do not come out. This phenomenon is only held by concentration. As soon as you relax a little, a multitude of thoughts will emerge again. Once again, you resume the process of "thought hunting" in the same way.

In this exercise we are trying to consciously find the mental process that enables us to muffle, suppress, destroy, or move a thought. Everyone can find a way to dissolve thoughts. Some will find this through a geographical point of focus in their mind; some will create a tension with a specific positioning of the eyes behind closed eyelids.

Part of the exercise is trying to understand exactly how you go about dissolving a thought rather than keeping a vague impression of it. Sometimes even facial muscles can tense up in the attempt to quieten a thought. It is important to notice all the details.

Eliminating thoughts is a relatively physiological process; you just have to find out how to go about it. As this creates tension, obviously, as soon as you begin to relax, all the hidden thoughts burst out. The only way to avoid this is to gradually find a way to eliminate the thoughts with the least possible tension so that the exercise can last longer.

Exercise 3: The shelter thought

Once you know how to physiologically make the thought/thoughts disappear, you want to keep one of them as your "shelter thought" and eliminate all the others. This means that as soon as another thought emerges, you can go back to your "shelter thought." This unique thought can be a concept, an idea, a word, an image, or an object. It is a bit like holding a lid over the multitude of thoughts while looking at one of them that came out. If others are able to slip from beneath the lid, by focusing on your first "shelter thought" the one that escaped will go back under the lid.

When you are able to do this you can move on to the fourth step—stillness, the white screen—below.

Exercise 4: Eliminating all thoughts, even the shelter thought

This creates a void, yet there is still tension during the exercise due to the active attention focused on eliminating every thought. It is not at all liberating and it requires some energy, just like holding a lid down for some time. This is why it creates tension.

This technique is very important and you have to experience this in order to become the one in charge again, using your mind as a tool, and not the other way around. By this direct experience you come to know that you are the boss. As long as this is not done, you have no way to realize that thoughts are there to serve you and should be used as tools. This is in fact a real battle with the ego, which little by little is crushed down to a more reasonable size! When you repeat this technique, over time there will be less tension or effort invested and it will become easier.

The first sign of having a calmed mind is that you no longer have inner comments when people talk to you. You are available to really listen.

When you reach the second part of Shen Gong realization (which we have not yet described in detail), there is no internal comment when you speak either. This process happens naturally.

Stillness, the white screen
When you hold down the thoughts for some time, it will eventually become almost effortless and something very interesting will appear: a blank will materialize, often white, in front of your closed eyes. This is comparable to "white noise." Nothing is happening. Stillness is the next step, bringing silence. This is described by the term "white screen." Some will describe it as if going through a warm shower or a cool shower, with the feeling of something letting go and a sense of tingling up and down the body. The beginning of mental silence comes at the end of the process of calming your mind. This can be an extremely long process if you have no guidance. With these guidelines, however, you can reach this state in just a few months if you practice every day. Once again, the guidelines are looking at your mind and learning how to hold your thoughts. Within this process you reach mental silence; the mind is calm except when we need to use it deliberately.

The "white screen" could almost be considered a moment "in between"—a space in which we linger between the thought we just suppressed and the next one coming. This time period will stretch and we can remain longer in this space where nothing is happening.

This is called the "small realization of Kan and Li" (the balance between Water and Fire), the balance and the contact point between the mind and the body. It is also said to be the center of the mind and the alignment on the world's Chong Mai, the spiritual axis. Many terms are used to explain this, but they all come from individual experiences, so the most important thing is to search for it personally.

The more you practice, the less frightening this experience will become. This will lead you to gradually stay longer in the state of "white screen," which will then also lead to very interesting physical and physiological sensations. The body's circulation tends to increase, the heartbeat slows down, and the breath is lengthened; all of these elements combine to convey a genuine feeling of wellbeing.

Of course, before achieving this you go through many moments of withdrawal, especially when you first start to experience this stage. You gradually stay longer. It is as if the fear of falling is transformed progressively into the desire to be in freefall, feeling yourself floating in the air. Many traditions compare this moment to mental levitation. It is a moment of absence.

> *Note: When we say that it is important to know yourself, this does not mean that at some point in the practice you are able to use more refined tools to analyze your mind. Analysis does not exist in Shen Gong practice. Once you practice, you will know at some point who you are just because you are. When you look at your hand, examining it does not make it more your hand. You know that it is your hand because it is your hand. You do not have to find ways to understand this. It is the same for who you really are.*

This brings us back once again to the name of our school—Da Xuan: the Great Secret. The great secret is not hidden. It is right in front of you, but you are in the dark and cannot see it. Once you put the right amount of light in that area, however, you can see it clearly. It is obvious and needs no analyzing.

Therefore, the first step in Shen Gong is accepting who we are. This is very hard if you have to force yourself to accept who you are!

We are naturally in rebellion against who we truly are. This is due to everything we have constructed, our own projection of who we are, our comparisons with others, our expectations, our fantasies linked to our belief system. All these aspects form a barrier. This barrier will dissolve little by little with the repetition of the practice. Even if you are aware of this barrier, you cannot confront it directly. You will never succeed using confrontation because this will create more tension. With gradual and constant repetition of this practice, however, the barrier of beliefs will slowly and naturally be replaced by other beliefs emanating from our true nature. It is the same idea with habits. It is extremely hard to get rid of a bad habit; when you try to do so, it creates a lot of tension and you think about it all the time. The only way is to replace it with another habit.

This difficulty in watching your mind can keep you from going further, so it is crucial not to give up. When you regularly connect yourself to the white screen, you come to a state of silence. In order to attain this, you must get past the obstacles set by your ego to prevent you from watching your mind and containing your thoughts. Unfortunately, these are the only ways to calm the mind.

What matters here is perseverance with no expectations. Do not look for results, sensations, or gratification. The positive aspect in Shen Gong is simply repeated practice. It is often the lack of results that turns people away from Shen Gong, when in fact it is the accumulation and time spent practicing that will lead you to a peaceful mind. Investing in loss is worth it because this effort, which is not in itself rewarding, will give you the ability to stop looking for results and to practice for the practice. This is the only possible evolution in Shen Gong.

It is not like physical training which can be rewarding with concrete results. In meditation, evolution will happen naturally, but there will not be immediate gratification. Nevertheless, there is something to look forward to, and this is the joy that it can bring which seeps into your daily life and into your interaction with other people. This joy comes from having an available mind—the consequence of a peaceful, calm mind. This is a natural process that you cannot force but comes with a daily practice. Signs of joy, enthusiasm, and desire are true signs of evolution in the practice of Shen Gong.

Shen Gong is purely mental and spiritual work. Its purpose is not simply to be relaxed. Yet it does have an effect on emotions. This is because our mind is not in accordance with our body. This creates friction—and thus emotions—so, in this sense, Shen Gong is indirectly physiological. However, real mind work is not material. The training is relaxing at first because it calms emotions, but this is not its main purpose. It is made to work on a spiritual level. It is a work on the immaterial and non-incarnated world. This is why after the first part of calming the mind comes the second part of self-realization, perfectly accomplishing our celestial destiny, and then comes the third part, going beyond and correcting what goes past our own destiny.

True happiness comes from within, with the desire and enthusiasm for life, directly linked to the Shen, the mind.

Chapter 5

Achieving Happiness by Occupying the Mind

Once we realize what our mind truly is, we want to occupy it. In order to keep it busy, we will work on the five senses, we will play with counting, and we will use images with contemplation.

1. Work on the five senses

This is often one of the most pleasant ways for people to train in Shen Gong. We mainly use the sense of hearing, more so than the sense of sight because the visual sense is directly linked to the mental mind and words. It is very hard to look without putting words on what you see, and in this action the mind is automatically activated. The sense of taste is more complicated to use. We can use touch, but it is not ideal since we are supposed to be completely still. Moreover, touch requires a major Yi projection which is directly linked to the mental mind.

Therefore, hearing is the sense used most appropriately in Shen Gong. You can project your hearing in practically any environment, and even the quietest places will never be completely silent. The fact of reaching out and seeking sounds gives the mind a real opening and you can let yourself get lost in this quest. Some systems actually produce sounds to be followed until they die down—bells, for instance.

Getting the mind's attention through a specific perception is exactly what we are looking for because the goal is to distract the mind. We bring it to a certain action—here, listening to sounds—and it will naturally calm the rest of the mind, thus calming the rising thoughts.

> *Note: When you use your senses to occupy the mind, you are not working on calming the mind. You are occupying the mind. All of the exercises comprised in the first part of Shen Gong leading to happiness can be practiced by anyone and not necessarily in a particular order. However, if you want to benefit from the specific nature of each exercise, it is preferable to follow their order. For instance, occupying your mind with the exercise on hearing will bring you the experience of dissociating the inside from the outside, your perception as opposed to reality. This capacity will only be possible once your mind is calm. So if you try to occupy your mind first, it may be pleasant, but you will not gain the same benefit from the exercise.*

2. Counting techniques

There is really nothing better to occupy the mind. You can count in your mind or on your fingers. You can count simply (from 1 to whichever number you end up with at the end your exercise) or with a rhythm (you choose a sequence—for instance, from 1 to 7—and repeat it until the end of the exercise). Or you can count with mixed numbers—for instance, 5–8–6–1. Usually, when the mind is distracted from these various sequences, you will end up counting normally again. Then you will have to go back to the chosen exercise.

There is also the countdown method: you count up to certain number and from there you count back down. And then start over again.

You can also mix all these counting techniques in order to make it even harder for the mind to follow. You can use your fingers, touching your thumb to a finger on the same hand at each count. You can touch your fingers one after the other, or every other finger with the corresponding number. Any pattern is possible.

By doing this, it is clear that your mind is empty of all thoughts, but only because it is distracted. Nevertheless, it does help the mind to get a grasp of the possibility for emptiness.

There is also the option of using a physical tool such as a rosary or mala. You can move your fingers to another bead at each breath or each time you are distracted from the focus of your exercise. Using these tools enables you stay still and silent and aligned.

> *Note: It is important to make the distinction between occupying the mind and distracting the mind. You occupy the mind with something clear and contained, using basic exercises. You stay focused because you are first and foremost in the practice, working on yourself. If you distract your mind, it is broader and not contained—watching TV, for instance. You are no longer in your practice because you are not conscious of yourself in this situation. Your mind is projected on to something else.*

You do not have to choose one of the techniques above and stick to it throughout your Shen Gong training. You can go from one exercise to another, as long as you know which part of the practice you are in—whether it is calming the mind or occupying the mind.

Also, these exercises must work for you. Some may create more tension than others. The training must be long enough so that you can switch from one exercise to another. You can even combine techniques, but it is better to try this once you know how to do each exercise separately.

Occupying the mind also brings a sort of tension which will decrease with time. This is a matter of repetition. When you practice Shen Gong, you burn a lot of energy and you also generate a lot of heat, so it is important to drink plenty of water before and after the exercise to nourish the Yin.

3. Images

The third way of occupying the mind is through images. Traditionally, it is said that we should only use images that do not have an analytical purpose. Ideally, we use seals, which are the equivalent of mandalas in our school. It is good to have the biggest seal possible so that the seal is the only thing in front of you.

The most complete practice for all aspects of the human being with the use of seals consists in losing yourself within the seal. First you need to relax the focus and then you let yourself go into the seal. In these types of exercises, instead of controlling, you let go. Often, because we are afraid of truly letting go, we will catch ourself and come out of the seal.

Where the first section—knowing your mind—brings a better awareness of what the mind is, the second section—occupying the mind—will truly start the process of taming the mind and recreating a genuine relationship, a friendly relationship, with our own mind.

Chapter 6

Achieving Happiness
by Focusing the Mind

In the first part of Shen Gong, the search was to know your mind; in the second part you worked on taming it. Now you want to use your mind in the proper way. The focusing exercises are important in learning how to use your mind as a tool. When you use your mind as a tool, it becomes a source of joy and wellbeing, both of which are related to the Shen.

1. Concentration

Often we use simple objects such as triangles, circles, or squares in order to keep the focus on something specific. As soon as our mind drifts off, we bring it back to the center by re-concentrating on the object. We should be able to do this for at least 30 minutes, although in fact it proves very hard to complete this exercise without being distracted by thoughts. It is also possible to do the same exercise without an object, simply using a mental focus, which we hold firmly in our mind. At first this is very demanding.

The best way to start is by picking a simple geometric form and a simple color. When you close your eyes, you create this image and you keep it all through the exercise without deforming it, making it move, or changing it, without interpreting it, and without drifting into other thoughts. Experience shows that the triangle works best, compared with the circle, which will bend out of shape more easily, or the square, which loses its proportions.

In Ba Zi (astrology), Feng Shui (geomancy), and in our tradition in general, there is no information on colors. Only in magic are colors mentioned. It is known that red, connected to fire and dynamism, is the easiest color to keep during the visualization, but try other colors if they work better for you. The main goal is to keep everything the same throughout the exercise.

This exercise consists in keeping in front of our closed eyes a simple geometric form and color. There is no emphasis on remaining still and silent. This work really develops our mental capacities for concentration. If this is too challenging at first, another option is to use a real image of a geometrical form in front of you. You keep the image in your mind, and when you feel you are losing it, you open your eyes, go back to the picture, and then close your eyes again. This should be easy to do, but the more your mind is in rebellion due to your inner conflict, the more it reveals a discrepancy between who you really are, who you think you are, and who you pretend to be. As a consequence, your mind is less stable and capable.

It might be difficult for some people to complete this exercise. It will depend on your ability to remember an image or even create and keep a mental image. However, anyone can accomplish this by first trying to keep the image of a real object in mind daily and then moving to the next step of creating a mental image. If you practice daily, you should be able to acquire this ability within a month or so. The length of time you are able to keep the image before your closed eyes is the most difficult part.

Once again, this requires effort and uses energy. It is very Yang and brings heat and dynamism, even though you might feel tired during it.

This type of technique is a genuine reflection of the relationship you have with your mind, whether you are in conflict with it or at peace.

2. Focusing

In order to practice focusing, we will use a concept. The concept you use can be anything from world peace to your pet animal. It does not matter. This is an open way of focusing. It automatically brings more information to mind that you will not have to suppress.

It remains difficult, though, since concepts mean something and are automatically associated with words, images, and thoughts. You can let them rise, but your focus stays on the concept. You do not analyze the rest.

The more the mind has to make an effort, the easier the chosen concept should be. It is helpful to choose something you like—for instance, if you are into soccer, go for a soccer ball, a soccer field, or a well-known player! It is only when you have an available trained mind that you can direct it towards important, broad, intangible concepts (love, death, empathy, violence).

Note: A concept is not an image in the sense that you do not automatically visualize your concept. It is not putting the concept into words either. This would be similar to the counting exercise, which is not the case here. It is very difficult not to see a mental image of your concept. This is why this exercise comes at the end of the training when you have developed your capacities through the techniques above. If you do it before you are ready, it will become an occupation for the mind, which corresponds only to the second part. The whole point of using a concept is your presence with the concept throughout the exercise. This calls for a balanced mind to be in the moment.

There is a point in the mind that enables us to be centered and aligned. It is represented in the Nei Jing Tu. When you train the mind, the first manifestation is the ability to focus on your activity and the amount of work you can accomplish in a short time. The second manifestation is your relationship to other people and your ability to listen.

These are two of the three steps that will bring joy to our mind, and hence to our lives.

The very last exercise that finalizes the steps to happiness through Shen Gong is something that seems easy but must be done for a longer period of time.

3. Open attention

To work this exercise, you hold your position, aligned, in silence and in stillness, and stay in the present attention of yourself without letting thoughts arise.

This open attention is presence in the moment. Be careful not to drift into thoughts and concepts. If you know how to keep a thought, an image, or a concept, you also know how to exclude them from your mind.

This capacity to be permeable to our own attention results from training with the techniques we have seen in the first, second, and third parts. This last exercise requires time—at least 45 minutes—in order to really experience the present moment.

Part Three

Introduction to Nei Dan
(Internal Alchemy)

Chapter 7

===

Lacking Energy and Building Energy

Nei Dan is inner alchemy—transformation of energy. If you compare inner alchemy with external alchemy, you will notice that when you are in the process of transformation, more often than not you end up having to stop the process because some specific ingredient is missing: there is never enough during the transformation process.

This is true with inner alchemy as well. We lack energy as our main ingredient. We are drawn to the work of inner alchemy because of its magical aspect. The idea of being able to transform the Yang is very attractive. But we forget that we are transforming an energy that is supposed to be our fuel for life. More often than not, this energy is not available because we are lacking it.

> *The energy used in Nei Dan is the leftover of what has been consumed in our daily life. So the energy used in inner alchemy is the excess. Inner alchemy can only work with a surplus of available energy; otherwise, we would be depleting our fuel fairly quickly!*

The good side of Nei Dan is that if you do not have a sufficient surplus of energy, the transformation will not work. So there is no risk of consuming your vital energy in the process. However, signs of missing energy will immediately appear during the practice. For instance, it can be manifested through lack of attention. This is not necessarily due to the fact that you are bored with the exercise; it is just that you do not have enough energy to focus. The problem occurs even in our daily life: we rarely have enough energy to get through the day. Often unhealthy eating habits and poor lifestyle (long working hours, too little sleep) will completely consume our existing energy and none will be spared for the transformation work.

The techniques to accumulate energy are very simple. Work on breath *is* work on vitality. Qi (energy) comes from what you eat and what you breathe (food and air). In fact, the simplified Chinese character for Qi only shows the air, as this is the most important aspect. Qi cannot be dissociated from breathing. Breath work is therefore intimately related to Qi. According to Yuan Nei Dan (the original Nei Dan), if you work the breath enough, the center will form and the energy will flow. So this implies that the circulation in Nei Dan techniques will happen naturally once the work on breath is trained and energy is sufficient.

However, the circulation will only occur if there are no blocks (body, mind, and emotions). Some training is required to make sure the blocks have dissipated. The main aid in getting rid of blocks is Shen Gong (work on the mind).

Later on we will see how training the small circulation in the stages of Nei Dan is very beneficial when you have excess energy available to be refined. But the process itself requires so much energy that it can only work after accumulating Qi through the work on breath. If the energy is insufficient, you will have to stop the process each time—in the same way that if your car runs out of gas, there is no way to keep on going until you add more gas.

Caution: One considerable waste of energy is all the fantasies and expectations linked to the work on energy!

We are just working on the breath. We want to become intimate with our breath. The goal is to practice breathing exercises every day and to remind ourselves as much as possible what it feels like to really breathe.

Important points before you begin
How do we go about gaining energy?
In Nei Dan, the main focus is on the breath. The breathing exercises will generate much more energy, producing an excess that will be available for the rest of the Nei Dan process.

When is the time to harvest?
Harvesting will be a period of time *before* you start your Nei Dan. Once you start the practice, you have to be in a place in which you have accumulated enough energy for the process to work. Just as in external alchemy when you harvest the plants you will be using, you make sure you have enough of each ingredient and that none has been lost while collecting them.

The main way to go about harvesting is to generate more energy on the one hand and, on the other, to adopt a way of life that will avoid wasting your energy.

There are several ways to go about changing your life habits during this harvesting period. All the major aspects of life should be examined: sleep, nutrition, work, social life, physical exercise.

The most important point to optimize your sleep is that you need a lot of it (you can survive on four hours, but it will certainly not regenerate your body, mind, and emotions). So getting a lot of sleep and going to bed before 10pm and waking up around 6am would be ideal.

As far as nutrition is concerned, you must choose food that carries the most Jing possible. It goes without saying that the fresher the better and that anything processed is out of the question. For instance, during this period you can follow a very strict Daoist diet. This consists in only eating what is unprocessed by man. So it excludes all cereals, but does include meat, fish, vegetables, and fruit. Changing your diet is not an obligation; in fact, all of the following are only suggestions. Nevertheless, you must be aware of what can help your endeavor and what can slow you down and tire you. Maintaining a regular work rhythm might be difficult because this is one of the aspects of life that takes the most out of us. This has to be a calm period with no strenuous or stressful work requirements. Being on holiday during this period would therefore be ideal.

With regard to your social life, partying all night is obviously not the best idea. Time spent on the phone, computer, and other interactions should also be cut down to those that are most important to you.

Finally, you must reconsider the type of physical activity you take on. Anything intense, although good for your heart and getting the circulation going, will use up a lot of energy.

Everything must be organized to accumulate the maximum energy before starting Nei Dan. If you lack energy the Nei Dan work will merely lead to *experiences* of inner alchemy; no real evolution or transformation will be achieved.

> *Imagine you are trying to boil water, but each time it is about to start boiling you take it off the stove—you will never get the water to transform into steam.*

The ability to keep the energy you have generated during training is developed later on. By then you will be able to exercise Qi Gong for a few minutes and keep every little bit of the energy generated.

But this also happens when you store a lot of energy. After a while the energy just stays and is not dissolved or consumed as easily. This is the system of thermodynamics. When you heat something that is already warm, the heat will stay longer and will generate more heat. If you try to heat something cold, the heat will rise and will dissipate quickly. So if you build up more energy on a base that is already strong energy-wise, it will stay. But it will not stay if the base is not solid, if energy is lacking, or if it is required for another activity. This is why building a solid base is crucial in order to accumulate energy, and hence why being attentive to our lifestyle and habits is important. We are so used to depleting our existing stock before the energy even has time to accumulate that we do not feel the extent of the damage until we start changing our habits. In the beginning, you might notice you need more sleep. Once you are more attentive to your needs, fatigue accumulated over the years manifests itself more clearly.

Protecting your Jing

If you use up your acquired energy, there will be no protective cushion left and soon you will be digging straight into your Jing (the innate Qi which is more or less strong depending on the person). Once the Jing is depleted, you die. So the goal is to build a big enough cushion to protect our Jing and never have to touch it.

The essence, Jing, is like a meter with a different number for each person (it's quite unfair!). When the meter runs down to zero, you die.

Each time you feel tired and you do not stop, each time you continue your activities instead of resting, it means you have used up your stock of Qi and are getting into the Jing. Normally, if you have enough acquired energy, you should never feel tired during your daily activities. Besides, in traditional Chinese medicine it is said that general fatigue is an illness. It is the syndrome of depleted Qi.

It is interesting to note how many times during the day we feel tired.

So the idea here is that even if you start out with very poor Jing (thanks, Mom and Dad!), it does not matter. Indeed, you can build a big enough cushion of acquired Qi to protect your Jing and never have to touch it. All these elements together are what can help generate more energy before starting Nei Dan. It is the idea that you must not spend your energy before building it. Let's say you have a bucket you want to fill with water. It is a problem if it has holes that let the water leak through. In this situation you can spend a lot of time trying to fill it up! So first you must make sure the base is solid and functional, and then you can start filling it up. And the way you live, the way you eat, the way you sleep, and, most importantly, the way you breathe, aligned with the principles above, will help build this solid base.

Qualifying energy

Qi is our vitality and it is what connects Man between Sky and Earth. This concept is based on the following rules:

- *You cannot quantify energy.* There is or there is not energy. If there is energy, it is sufficient and total. It cannot be measured. No matter where you are, energy is the same. There is no more energy at the top of a mountain than in a cellar, on the highway, or in the desert; energy is the same everywhere, no matter how high, cramped, or open the setting is.

- *There is no quality to energy.* You will not find a better-quality energy depending on where you are. If you are facing beautiful scenery, it might be more agreeable and might affect you on an emotional level, but it does not change the quality or the nature of the energy. And, on the other hand, if you are in a city at work in a cubicle, it might not be the most agreeable setting for you, but still the energy will be exactly the same. Energy is the same everywhere, no matter how pure or polluted the air is. In high altitude there is less oxygen, near the ocean more humidity, in the city more pollution, and this might indeed have an effect on the way you feel when you breathe (and on your lungs if you do your breathing exercises on the side of the freeway!), but it does not alter the energy.

Our school encourages the use of elements to make the work more pleasant. Therefore, choosing a setting you like is a good thing. But keep in mind that this is only to satisfy your emotions.

Energy and emotions

The body is linked to the essence, Jing, whereas thoughts are linked to the mind. Emotions, however, are linked to energy. Qi is in between the manifested and the non-manifested, just as Man is between Sky and Earth. Emotions, through breath, are materialized in the body as a manifestation of Qi (as opposed to thoughts, which are not manifested). This is why we say that Qi is emotion and represents Man. In other words, the work on breath is the practice most representative of humanity through its connection to Qi between Sky and Earth. In fact, at first our school only developed the breath work called Yuan Nei Dan. Then came the exercises to strengthen the body, and finally the exercises to soothe the mind.

Jing is also connected to the Earth, with its instinctive and material aspect. Shen is linked to the mind, being spiritual and intuitive. Qi is the interaction between Shen and Jing. When the spark from Yuan Shen (original spirit, absolute Yang) is incarnated in the first Jing cells (absolute Yin) to create a human being, it gives a movement. This movement is Qi.

> *Therefore, the work on Qi is the most human of all. Qi is the center of the work.*

Nevertheless, as a human being we must work on the totality of what we are, which includes our animal side and our spiritual side. Due to their connection, one can understand how energy can be tainted by emotions. This is why, in the later stages, the school added Shen Gong to the practice, in order to be more neutral during the breath work and not be overwhelmed by thoughts, which then become emotions. Therefore, if you can set a positive mood no matter where you are—freeway, overheated bedroom, or Grand Canyon—the exercise itself will have exactly the same value energetically. As long as you are in a place that seems OK to you, and you don't complain and whine, your breathing exercise will be perfect as it is.

You must also be in a positive state of mind to focus on your breathing. Otherwise, very quickly you will easily be disturbed by elements of your surroundings: the car honking down the street, your neighbor's dog barking, and so on. This requires being open and positive so as not to spoil the breath exchange with negative thoughts, which will taint your emotions, and hence your energy and your breath. This is the main reason each practice in our school is dependent on all the others.

If your body is weak, not grounded, or tired, you will not be able to be aligned and sit straight, and therefore you will not be able to breathe. Nor can you work properly if your mind is rambling on with comments and judgments. Every aspect of the Three Treasures must be trained equally: body, mind, and energy.

What are you training?

Do not get the goals mixed up. It is important to understand what you are training. Is it the mind with Shen Gong? Is it emotions? Are you trying to calm them or let them come out? Are you training the body and, if so, to reinforce it, to be aligned, or to be relaxed? Are you trying to feel energy or trying to build and store energy?

These are important questions as they will set the frame for your training. It is very easy to get confused. For instance, while doing your Shen Gong practice you can often slide into Nei Dan without even noticing it. If you start to focus on your breath instead of just the mind, this means you are no longer in the non-manifested realm but in the body because the breath is materialized in the body.

It is interesting to understand more profoundly the meaning of breathing on an energetic and spiritual level; however, you must not be overwhelmed by this during your practice. These are elements to take into account before starting the practice, but the focus during the exercise remains purely on breathing.

Besides, thinking of the meaning of breathing during the exercise would imply commenting. When you work on the mind, the comments are an element of distraction, which divert you from the work. In the breathing exercises, however, it goes further: the comments will be using part of your energy, so instead of generating more, you will be doing the opposite. You can see in that sense how any sort of visualization technique is out of the question during breathing exercises, as this would automatically consume more energy. Visualization may bring you an emotional boost, but it derives from a consumption of energy. This is something positive as long as your goal is not to store energy.

It is important to remind yourself what you are working on. It would be a pity, for instance, if, in wanting to generate energy, you opted for jogging! Many people think this brings energy. In fact, there is a difference between, on the one hand, generating and storing energy and, on the other, using energy in a way to help the body maintain a good circulation and thus develop muscular dynamism. This is why it is crucial to know what you are training, whether it is your emotions, your mind, or your vitality. This will help you improve your training because, first, you will choose the appropriate exercises and, second, your focus will be on the right element.

Chapter 8

Breathing Techniques and Exercises

At first, focusing on your breathing can be a tedious task and is not very stimulating. However, very quickly (after a week of 30 minutes' daily practice) you will undoubtedly feel more vitality. By continuing this process, energy will be stored for a better use. Simply breathing consciously is sufficient to activate the process.

There are techniques to breathe consciously and to help stay focused during the exercises. In this chapter we will present the foundation of the breathing work.

The balance of Yin and Yang

There is a perfect balance in breathing. When you inhale, it creates an effort for the body as the diaphragm contracts. The action here is more Yang; however, the breathing is Yin. When you exhale, the body relaxes, thus making the action more Yin, but the breathing itself is Yang. If you look at the Tai Ji, the Yin–Yang symbol, you will notice that there is always a bit of Yin in the Yang and a bit of Yang in the Yin.

These bits are, in fact, the pauses in between the action of breathing in and breathing out.

When you inhale, it is a Yang action but the breath is Yin, and the pause is a suspended moment when the Yin transforms into Yang. The exhaling is Yang, but the pause at the very end is the suspended moment when the Yang transforms into Yin.

Just like the Tai Ji, in which you have the Yang with a dot of Yin and the Yin with a dot of Yang, the pause consists of two stages: the Yang when the pause rises with the inhalation and the Yin when it falls with the exhaling. The rupture between the Yang and the Yin is that moment of eternity.

Decomposing the pause is a bit like trying to see when a train starts moving: either it is at a stop or it is in motion. But there is an in-between! It is the non-existence of time. This is why it remains a mystery: we cannot grasp it. It is similar to the moment you fall asleep. So when you think you are in the middle of the pause, you are in fact retaining the beginning or the end of it.

After a normal exhalation the body should let go. This is when the pause begins. At the end of the pause there is a dynamic interaction between principles, which triggers the beginning of the inhalation. This is the vital force that makes you start breathing in again. It is interesting to note that this vital force is within the pause. In between the letting go and the vital force, there is this mysterious moment.

The balance between inside and outside

At each breath cycle there is a perfect balance between the inside and the outside. With each breath you will bring energy in from the outside and reject used energy, thus cleaning the inside. The more you are conscious of your breathing, the more this exchange is beneficial, because it takes on a real meaning. On the other hand, if you have a short, unconscious breath, you will not be able to benefit from this exchange in the same way.

At each pause after breathing in you will come to realize you are nourished from the outside, and at each pause after breathing out you will become aware of how your body is cleaning itself out. This exchange is the connection of Man between Sky and Earth.

When you inhale, you accept part of the world according to the perception you have of it (tainted by your emotions); when you exhale you clean out what was inside your body. Both of these actions are manifested. The pauses in between are not.

In our school's breathing techniques to acquire vitality (before the Nei Dan work), these pauses are very important. In some texts it is said that these pauses are a link to the prenatal (Wu Ji), the non-manifested, "the mysterious passage."

> *Each breath is a relation between us towards the world, from the world towards us, and pauses, which remind us of immensity, immortality, and eternity.*

Position and posture

Before starting the exercise you must be aligned, still, and comfortable. Very quickly, posture will not be as important, nor will your daily activities affect your Nei Dan. At first, however, in order to build up a surplus of energy, you must consume the minimum amount of energy in your posture. If you are not aligned, there will be more friction and therefore more use of energy. If you feel pain or heat in specific parts of your body when you are seated, this will also be a misuse of energy. Furthermore, thoughts and complaints about the pain you are feeling are another cause of loss of energy. And your judgment on the thoughts you may have concerning that specific pain is yet another waste of energy! The possibilities of wasting energy are endless! You can see how every aspect developed above in relation to your posture can affect your energy.

This is why it is important to exclude all elements that you know may undermine the process. Keeping an aligned, comfortable posture will minimize the risks of energy misuse.

Besides, staying still brings more calmness because it reduces mental activity, and this allows the inner comments to decrease as well.

In your sitting position it is best to keep your legs bent and parallel, cross-legged, or a mix of both with one leg in front and one on the side. It is not recommended to keep your legs straight out in front as this causes a loss of energy. The legs should be bent at the guas (hip joints) and knees.

Finding the right position is harder on a chair than on the floor. Take a look at the statues of Buddha and see all the various positions he takes. You can even do the exercise lying down on your side (fetal position), although then you have a greater chance of falling asleep.

The limitations of seated exercises

In order to generate energy through seated breathing exercises, the body has to be strong and relaxed, which implies not having any blocks or troubles. Of course, this is rarely the case. In fact, the body, as it usually is, is not ready to generate that kind of energy just by sitting down. The body has to be prepared beforehand with physical work.

So, at first, Nei Gong is a more efficient way to gain energy. This is the physical work on energy linked to simple movements, which do not require your mental focus. The attention is set on the sensation and the breathing. This generates energy while relaxing the body and the mind.

Unless the body and the mind are relaxed, Nei Dan work is not possible.

Indeed, the breathing work is the center of all training, but it requires the other aspects of the practice—mind and body— in order to be balanced. This is very important, because if the structure cannot hold in the energy—if the bucket is pierced—it is going to be hard to gain any energy! Nevertheless, when you work standing up, a part of the generated energy will be redistributed automatically to reinforce your body, tendons and muscles, skin and fascia. Therefore, it is not possible to store the energy in the same way as sitting down.

The solution is to keep training in Nei Gong as well as doing seated breathing exercises. Ideally, you can check your posture in a mirror or even film yourself. You will be surprised how much you move and become unbalanced without even noticing it throughout the exercise. And the camera will not lie!

Exercise 1: Natural breathing

The breathing rhythm must be natural. You cannot force it, nor can you try to extend your breath. By breathing normally, each breath will extend naturally. For this you must be sitting in a comfortable position, still, and just start breathing while being aware of each breath. You do not want to manipulate your breath, however. You cannot force it. The breath must be silent to others and to yourself. Just this effortless action can be a source of anxiety because we are not used to watching ourselves breathe.

> If and as long as this exercise is difficult, you must not move on to another technique. You have to continue training your breath until it becomes natural.

As for the mind, either you are able to be in nothingness, thanks to Shen Gong work, and complete the exercise with no inner judgment, or, if this is not the case, you can occupy your inner judge by commenting on each breath with the word "inhale" when you inhale, and "exhale" when you exhale. Also, leave one second of pause between the moment you breathe in and breathe out.

The goal is to be able to experience *one* perfect breath cycle—in and out, soundless, balanced, with a pause. When you have done this, you repeat the process. It is better to do a series of breathing being perfectly focused, even if your mind then wanders off, rather than to try to do everything perfectly. Because that will *not* work! It will just create more tension and cause more energy to be wasted.

Also, in order for the exercise to work, you need a general preparation: for instance, you need to experiment with the best position before the practice, because once you start, if you keep testing your position, you will lose your main focus. All the little matter-of-fact details (blowing your nose, turning off your cellphone, scratching that mosquito bite) should be dealt with before starting the exercise so your mind can be free to focus solely on your breath. Therefore, you must be still, aligned, and comfortable. Inhale, pause, and exhale (you can add the comment on each action). When it works, you repeat the same thing. If you are unable to do this exercise relaxed for at least 30 minutes, this should be the only area of focus. Nevertheless, once in a while you can still test other techniques just to have an idea of where you are heading.

This first exercise should really be considered as a test. If you pass, you can continue with the rest of the progression. Otherwise, the rest should not concern you because you would not be able to evolve and gain energy through the other techniques.

Exercise 2: Breathing with counting

In order to understand how to count, you must first experiment with counting while you inhale and while you exhale. The counting rhythm is what comes naturally. There is no recommended speed; it just has to be your natural way of counting—for some people it will be faster than others. You then have an approximate number for each action. Once you see how long it takes you to breathe in and out naturally, you can apply that same count to your exercise and decide the exact number you will count to for each breath. At the end of each count, you count to three for your pause and then resume your counting. For instance, the pattern can be eight counts when you breathe in, three for the pause, eight when you breathe out, and again three counts for the pause. The inhaling and exhaling are usually fairly equal in length, but for some people one may be longer than the other. If that is the case for you, do not force them to be equal. Follow the numbers you have established for each action and always count to three or four for the pauses in between. Although the pause is slightly forced, you should not end up holding your breath. The pause exists naturally, but when you become aware of it and realize it is directly linked to the gate of immortality (the possibility to experience unity), obviously the pause will stretch out a bit! This second exercise requires you to slightly alter your breathing pattern, but in no way will this create problems. Once you have established precise counts, you want to keep the same pattern throughout the exercise.

Note: While respecting your breathing pattern, you may feel the need at some point to take a deeper, longer breath. This is due to the fact that your breathing cycle is probably not complete: either you do not let go enough when you breathe out or you are lacking the vital impulse when breathing in. In both cases, this creates tension and the long breath is a way to release. The inhalation begins with an increase of the vital impulse, then stabilizes with the air intake, and finally transforms. But the source of both breathing in and out is the pause. When you are not familiar with breathing techniques, you rarely go as far as the letting-go part which leads to the pause; therefore, you never reach the vital impulse either. This is specifically what must be trained, because when you breathe normally and unconsciously you do not reach this point of letting go. Once you are able to completely let go and experience the impulse, you are ready to die and live at each breathing cycle. When you are not able to let go and are caught up in the need for bigger breaths, this is purely the manifestation of fear—fear of falling asleep, of disappearing, of death, of life, and the fear of succeeding.

The good news is that this fear can completely disappear with the combined work on breath, body, and mind. This process will actually happen through breath work. Indeed, breath is connected to energy and emotions. It is the link between what is manifested (emotions) and what is not (energy). Through breathing, you materialize clinging thoughts into emotions, turning Yang into Yin. Also, the other way around, the breath will dissolve the Yin and transform it into Yang.

The first practice is very different from the second. The first one is simple in that there is no action except the focus on breathing. You can also reinforce your focus by mentally describing each action with the sentence "Breathe in, breathe out." In this second technique there is the effort in counting. This effort will distract the mind from its train of thought and will help focus on the breathing more efficiently. The downside is that it makes the exercise more demanding and tiring. Both techniques described above have in common the capacity of calming the mind while developing vitality. Here, vitality is the idea of having more energy but also being alive and accepting death as part of life.

Exercise 3: Follow the breath

This is the best and most complete of all breathing exercises. In fact, this is what Buddha did. Sitting still and comfortably, you want to focus on the sensation of your breath. Focus the attention on your nostrils, feeling the air come in when you inhale and following its passage. Do the same when you exhale. When you inhale, you will feel the air going down into the chest and you may even have the impression that it goes down to the center. It is important, though, not to follow the path as this would give a direction to your focus and bring you back to the center. This would become another exercise: heating the center! You just want to stay focused on one point and stick to it during the entire exercise. We have moved from soothing and counting techniques to kinesthetic techniques. Working on sensation is perfect for our goal, because when you are focused on the feeling in your body you do not consume energy. Simply being attentive to the sensation is different from using your intention to try to feel something. For instance, energy will be used when you try to bring the energy to your hand and feel it.

When the air goes in and out of the nose, this creates a sensation. You simply have to focus on that sensation and follow it. The air comes in when you inhale, the air goes out when you exhale, and in between there is always that little pause. Even though you can follow the movement and volume of air intake, it is best to focus on one point. Usually, the focus is on the lower tip of the nostrils or the middle or base of the nose, but some people prefer the palate or the throat. In any case, you want to keep the same point of focus during the entire exercise. There is a pause here but it is natural. Even when you do not feel it, there is always a pause when we breathe. The less you are familiar with this type of exercise, the more your breath will be short and superficial, and the less you will feel this pause. The fact of focusing your attention on the transition between breathing in and out actually lengthens the pause and you will become aware of it. Nevertheless, it remains natural, unlike the counted pause in the earlier exercise.

> *Once again, in natural breathing the pause exists, but if you force it, it becomes holding your breath.*

When you inhale, you feel the air entering, and you feel you are coming to an end when the air starts to thin. It is only when it has completely faded that you exhale. You are granting yourself the time to feel the pause in between this flow that increases with an impulse and decreases by letting go. It is interesting to make a parallel between the impulse and the letting go on the one hand, and the Hun (intuitive, spiritual) and the Po (instinctive, letting go) on the other. Furthermore, we can relate the action of starting the exercise to the Yin (intention) and the capacity to stay focused with the Zhi (the will). And here again we have the main axes of the Human Map. This Map is actually a guide to breathing. Within the Human Map you find curves that actually represent the breathing cycles and relate to the root of the tensions and origin of the vitality, which have things to reveal concerning breathing.

The tricky aspect of this technique is that, by following the sensation, there will be a tendency to increase the volume of air you inhale in order to feel it even better. This would be going against the natural aspect of breathing. This is something you can avoid by reminding yourself that the breathing has to be silent. When you can hear your breathing, this means you have increased the volume and the flow. In fact, there is no need to amplify the breathing in order to feel it; you just need to be more focused.

This technique is perfection in itself. It consumes no energy, it calms the mind, it fights boredom (you cannot be focused on two things at once, so if you are attentive to the sensation you cannot feel bored), and it feels good because each time you breathe in and out you are celebrating life! It is a real source of joy.

So this technique can actually be a real practice of Nei Dan. Once you have acquired the qualities through this technique, training the qualities will bring transformation. Then the Small Circulation and Great Circulation will simply be elements to test and add on; there will be no blocks and the energy will already be available, so everything will go smoothly. If you realize during the exercise that you are preparing your shopping list instead, just go back to the breathing sensation. Whatever you do, do not comment on your lack of attention: this would just be another waste of energy.

If you are lost in the sensation and find you are following the path of the air, just go back to the point you selected at the beginning of the practice. If this is too hard, you can start by using a product that brings a tingle to the spot—for instance, you can add a bit of mint oil at the tip of your nostrils if that is the place on which you will be focusing. In Nei Dan practice, distractions are not such a problem because we already have our base to work on, whereas here we are building our base by generating vitality. The distraction will immediately use part of that energy. Here, distractions are a real problem and this is why the kinesthetic focus is crucial to save you from distraction. Remember that the kinesthetic work is what is farthest from the mental process, thus farthest from the thought form.

Observing without investing yourself: Staying centered

The reason we do not open our eyes during these breathing exercises is because whatever you see can be used as a mental object and becomes a source of thought and comment. Opening your eyes brings more distraction. You may feel more relaxed with your eyes open, but this is only because you are less attentive to the exercise.

There is special training to achieve contemplation, which is observing without projecting thoughts or comments, without being invested in what you see. Our approach to reach this is working on the center in Nei Dan. When you work on your center, you work on the center of things; when you are at the center of things, you become aware of them and become part of them as well. You become porous, and even with your eyes closed you can observe the outside through your entire body (these are techniques based on breathing through your skin in the Great Circulation).

> It is interesting to note that the center of the pause is related to your own center, itself related to the center of everything, and if you are everything, you dissolve into nothingness, just like the "mysterious way" in the center of the pause.

When you have been working on breath for a long time, you notice that you breathe not just through your nose but through your entire body as well, which then conveys the feeling of being permeable to all elements, just like a thin veil. When you breathe out far and breathe in close, the envelope that separates the outside and your center no longer exists. This is known as "extending and condensing," and elements go through you because you are part of everything. At this stage it is a great opportunity to train outdoors in order to feel the wind actually going through you. Of course, this is not what actually happens physically, but the sensation cannot be better described!

Exercise 4: Preparing the ultimate exercise

We are still focusing on the sensation of the air on a specific zone. But here you will stay on the pause a little longer. This means that you are almost holding your breath during the pause, but as soon as you realize you are holding the air in, you let go. So it is a very light retention of air. You only do this when you breathe in, not when you breathe out.

> *The rhythm goes as follows: breathe in, hold your breath for barely a second, consciously breathe out, and naturally breathe in with no conscious pause.*

This amplifies the inhalation consciously, but in fact it lengthens the exhalation as well. This specific way of holding in the air on an inhalation is one of the only techniques that has no negative effects. On the contrary, it is actually used therapeutically in Daoist medicine.

If this method is too demanding and requires too much attention, just try to do a few cycles perfectly and relax by simply following the sensation as in Exercise 3.

Exercise 5: Developing vitality

This is the most simple, free, and open exercise of all, yet the hardest!

You just want to be conscious of the fact you are breathing at every inhalation and exhalation. You no longer focus on a specific sensation, but simply become aware of your natural breathing. In fact, more than being focused, this requires an open and conscious attention. This of course implies a calm mind and a relaxed body since there is no technique to occupy them in this method. The commentator will not be distracted with counting, nor will the body and mind be occupied with kinesthetic work. There is no artifact to calm you down.

This seems like the easiest exercise as there is nothing to do, but really the fact of not having any instructions or details makes it much more difficult to hold your attention. If you are able to maintain a stable attention, there will be no consumption of energy and you will be generating energy. This technique alone can build the center and the circulations in Nei Dan.

This is a very good alternative for people who have trouble with heating the center using the work on points. Instead of trying to direct the energy to specific points to trigger the circulation, here we will simply generate a lot more energy and let it distribute naturally. In all the exercises above, you might already feel the center heating. That's fine, but always make sure to come back to the initial focus required by the technique. All the exercises above prepare for this final technique. It is based on all the others, but it is free and can either bring you a lot if you stay attentive or bring you nothing—zero—if you are distracted.

The relaxed and free aspects of this technique make it much more pleasant, but you can also end up daydreaming! That is the risk of the openness of this technique. But all our other tools developed through Shen Gong, Nei Gong, Wai Gong, and Qi Gong will be very useful here. The trouble with all these methods is that they are directly linked to our emotions; usually when we first start, we feel anxiety, which is due to the realization of what it means to breathe. Basically, if you stop breathing, you die! This will pass; however, all the other emotions will rise up. Sometimes even the posture can trigger the rise of a specific emotion.

This is why the Xin Yi Dao Yin Fa, the work on emotions, is also very useful while training in Nei Dan.

This breathing technique is the one that will bring the most vitality with the least consumption of energy. This is the one technique that brings you to the "great breathing." This complete form can be a genuine Nei Dan. It is a Nei Dan of realization rather than a Nei Dan with conscious actions. By practicing this technique, evolution will happen naturally; gradually, without pushing it in any particular direction, the Small Circulation will develop and move up to the Great Circulation. The Nei Dan, as we usually know it, is called the Way of Fire. It is an active Nei Dan with intent. It is very much linked to the Path of the Warrior.

The Great Breathing is a Nei Dan called the Way of the Wind. Here the only action is to generate and store more energy in the system, without intention. The system will then naturally accomplish the cycles of circulation by using the surplus of energy. Not only is this in itself a complete way of Nei Dan, but it is also a great exercise to calm and soothe the body and the mind through abandonment.

If your attention and intention are clear, you can do anything.

Part Four

Introduction to
Xin Yi Dao Yin Fa
(Cultivating Emotional Energy)

Chapter 9

What Can Be Said Without a Teacher

Xin Yi Dao Yin Fa is more complex to practice: you need to practice with a teacher because emotions need to be explained before they can be tamed.

The trick with emotions is that you need to feel them when they manifest as physiological changes and, even better, as Qi movement. To do that, we need to be aware of the changes that emotions provoke in our system.

Exercise 1: Emotion

Each time you experience a strong emotion, look at and feel the different physical tension that you may experience. Note this and link it to your emotion.

After a while you will realize that each emotion has the same manifestation for you, which is maybe not the same for another person.

Exercise 2: Tension

Each time a tension comes to the place of emotions that pick up from everyday frustrations, each time a place in your body is tense, try to relate it to the emotion you know.

Look for the Qi movement before this tension—before the emotion revealed itself.

Exercise 3: "Dead" or stuck

Doing Nei Gong, energy work, and energy awareness, you may feel that some part of your defensive energy is "dead" or stuck—less alive.

Are these dead places related to the strong invading emotions you experienced?

After this preparation, you need to see a teacher for these Xin Yi Dao Yin Fa practices. They are rare and precious teachings, and you may have to search for a good teacher.

> *The breath and Qi work and experience are the key to the emotional work. If you practice the other exercises of Qi, the emotional work will be easy when you meet the right teacher.*

Part Five

Deepening Our Practice (Revealing the Complete Map of Da Xuan Daoism)

Chapter 10

The Eighteen Methods Leading
to the Gates of Madness

The work on the mind is based on three stages:

1. Calming the mind

2. Dissociating

3. Uniting.

In these three great concepts, the idea is to train the mind to make it available; this is the main goal as a student of the practice. You must have an available mind to understand the Way, to learn and comprehend the concepts, and to practice well. If your mind is not available, it will filter most of the teachings and it will be impossible to practice well.

Furthermore, from an energy standpoint, the constant flow of unnecessary thoughts and our continuous judgments and comments use up a great amount of energy, even more than the body uses.

In traditional Chinese and Daoist medicine it is said that internal illnesses—unbalances due to the mind and emotions—are the primary cause of premature death. Therefore, it is absolutely necessary to start training the mind and taking care of it.

The practice of Shen Gong, just like the practice of Nei Dan, strives for a certain ideal of accomplishment. The level of accomplishment evolves with the stages of practice. The first goal is to calm the mind.

1. Calming the mind

This is the first step and the most important one for the student; unless this process is completed, there can be no further evolution in the practice. There are very precise techniques to train this first stage. We call them the Eighteen Methods Leading to the Gates of Madness. Training with these methods will lead to happiness. What we call happiness is not based on external factors (possessions, family, professional accomplishments). Here, happiness is an inner perception of the world. This is a constant state of happiness developed with the first part of Shen Gong work—that is, calming the mind. It corresponds to basic meditation in Buddhism.

> Note: Meditation in Shen Gong is purely mental; it is not linked to the breathing process. In our school, this would be considered a mistake, in the sense that breathing is a physical aspect. If you meditate by following your breath, you are focusing your attention on something physical and not solely on mental activity. If your focus of attention is on the breath, and thus vitality, then it becomes Nei Dan work.

There is a difference between, on the one hand, the physical, the matter, the body, and, on the other, the mind, which is intangible. The mind does not exist. It is only manifested physically through emotions. A calm, balanced, and available mind makes you happy. Everyone is interested in this ability because it implies no more suffering! And this is also what makes it so important to study the basic functioning of the mind and to train this first stage through the Eighteen Methods. This first part is qualified as "training the mind."

2. Dissociating

This is the equivalent to deep meditation. The idea is to push the mind into a union with the two other Treasures: the body and the Qi, the breath. This second training of dissociating consists of Eight Meditations to Conquer Your True Nature. This stage leads to realization—that is, the accomplishment of your real nature with the possibility to completely fulfill your potential. As you will have already noticed, there is a clear distinction made between the first stage that leads to true inner happiness and the second stage. The main reason for this distinction is that you can very well accept and go along with your little problems and flaws and still be happy. This really is the first stage of calming the mind.

In this second part, we will focus the work on clarifying the aspects of the mind in order to reach a realization accomplishment. This second part is qualified as "developing the mind until its accomplishment."

3. Uniting, returning to oneness

This third major cycle of Shen Gong is practiced with a method called Passing through the Nine Circles to go beyond Life and Death. When you start this stage of the practice, you are already accomplished as you went through the second stage of dissociation. This means that you will go beyond what you are as a fully accomplished human being, pushing further than your manifested nature. At this point you have gone into the spiritual, esoteric world. This third part is qualified as "transforming the mind." There is transformation because you perfect and sublimate your nature as a human being.

Chapter 11

The Nine Words of Guidance

Fortunately, there are words of caution and guidance throughout the practice in order to help situate oneself within Shen Gong evolution. This is also a way to find answers to the major questions in relation to your level of practice. These words, like most of the teachings, used to be learned by heart by the student.

Following are the Nine Words of Guidance for the student of Shen Gong:

I.   The Five Requests to Set a Proper Training

II.   The Three Levels of Practice of the Mind (in the second stage)

III. The Nine Levels of Realization (in the third stage)

IV.   The Thirty-Five Stages on the Path to the Mind

V.   The Eight Steps to Evolution of the Mind

VI.   The Three Impossibilities and Four Dangers

VII. The Three Purities and Nine Chances

VIII. The Six Advices of the Realized Man

IX.   Don't Be Afraid.

All of these words of guidance work in the same direction to calm, separate, and unite the mind. The mind needs to be available, then clarified, reunited, and connected to the Yuan Shen.

I. The Five Requests to Set a Proper Training

These can be interpreted on several levels of understanding. Some aspects are very basic and others really profound: from very functional, physical notions to mysterious, esoteric notions. Hence there are many levels of reading! These are really good to learn by heart because once you understand what these little sentences signify, you then use them according to what they really mean to you.

1. Be quiet!

This can simply be linked to being in action rather than in a discussion, since the practice is linked to action. Also, the practice requires experience, and experience is not acquired through discussion but through the action of training. "Be quiet" is also meant for your mind that never stops talking—the inner judge who comments on everything.

2. Practice every day

Every day means *every* day! There is no exception. Take the image of a pot of water that needs to boil. It will only boil if you leave it long enough. It is a process. If you keep turning off the fire, even for a few seconds, the water won't come to the boil. Following the same idea, it is said that a day of training is a day of training, but one day without is *ten* lost days. It may be an exaggeration, but the idea remains true! Furthermore, there is a time of internal maturation between each exercise. This is because from one Shen Gong exercise to the next the mind has time to accept, understand, and assimilate certain aspects of the training and evolution. However, the longer you wait between each exercise, the harder it is to get back into the specific state that it requires.

If you attain a certain state with 10–15 minutes' daily practice, you will see that as soon as you stop this daily rhythm, it will be much harder to get back into the same state. If you practice every day, you can stay lazy and practice less. Eventually, the practice will become part of your day rather than being ritualized. You will not need to practice as long, because fairly quickly—within a few seconds or minutes—you will be in the right state to resume training. Practicing every day in the long term brings perfection to the practice in less time!

3. Ask a question after one week of reflection

This is not only with regard to your teacher or other students. It also applies to yourself, when your thoughts and comments on your practice trigger questioning. Often, by letting a week go by, while continuing to practice, your questions will be answered naturally or they may no longer seem relevant. The idea here is to keep thoughts and questionings from polluting your daily practice. By letting a week go by, you do not build up pressure or mobilize the mind, trying to find an answer. Giving yourself this time opens up the possibilities for answers. Therefore, the best way to confront an interrogation is to be quiet and practice.

4. Respect the sources of evolution

This is your own evolution and also the evolution of your practice. The sources come from the teachings, the teacher, the school, but also from your fellow students of the Way. The importance you give to these actors will enable you to clarify your practice. Obstacles within these relationships will block your practice. The priority as a student of the Way is the teaching and what enables evolution. This implies keeping petty attitudes regarding one another from interfering with the practice. Thus, only by respecting what qualifies as the Way are you able to evolve. On a more subtle level, it also implies letting go. This is an essential component of Shen

Gong—much more than Nei Dan, much more Yin than Shen Gong, and not at all required in the physical work.

5. Hold yourself, respect yourself

This is the concept of not letting yourself fall into any sort of strategy of failure—for instance, stopping your practice as soon as things go well or being driven by destructive behaviors which keep you from practicing. You have all the concepts to practice well and it is up to you to respect yourself, to hold yourself, and to adopt a conduct that enables you to practice. This is the hardest notion of all five because it is intimately linked with the dark zones of the Human Map.

II. The Three Levels of Practice of the Mind (in the second stage)

1. Training the mind

The first level, the training of the mind, comes from the development of the mind's qualities.

The search for a balanced mind, as represented in the Human Map, is what leads to a stable state of happiness. It is the ability to perceive the world differently. For this purpose, we use the Eighteen Methods Leading to the Gates of Madness to train the mind.

Why do we use the term "Gates of Madness"? In some respects, an accomplished student of the Way is separated from the rest of the world. It is something that makes him different. Often people will mock him. When you apply a strict discipline to various aspects of your daily life, the majority of people will not approve or be supportive. On the contrary, they will often try to divert you from this imposed discipline. Therefore, this attitude will create a friction rather than a feeling of shared happiness.

This is an unfortunate reflex due to the fact, first of all, that people want attention; second, they often wish they could also have a disciplined life but are not willing to act on it. Why should you have something they don't? Therefore, for all these reasons we see that "madness" mainly means difference. Nevertheless, although the training creates a difference, this difference is what leads to happiness.

As much as the world can be a source of agitation, it still remains healthy since our goal is to live within society. However, the calming and soothing of a united mind and the ability to perceive the world differently do create a distance between us and the world in which we live.

2. Developing the mind

The second level, developing the mind, is trained with the Eight Meditations to Conquer Your True Nature. Here we talk about the opening of our spiritual center (Ni Wan Gong). This is the process of realization—to be truly accomplished as a human being.

Whereas in the first stage you develop the qualities to have a balanced and united mind, in this second part you develop what we call the "powers." These are not superpowers! These are the powers that you find in the Human Map, such as the ability to see the world change, real clarity, and so on. These powers allow your innate capacities to be revealed. Most people naturally have one or two powers. Once the mind is cleared and open to the world (when the mind is calmed and united, and you have acquired true happiness), your true self and these innate capacities will be revealed naturally (Zin Ran).

Although there are levels for these eight meditations, you can train in them even if you are not at the appropriate stage. During these meditations you will have experiences that can benefit the training. This can be explained with the concept of states of consciousness as opposed to stages of evolution. With certain techniques you can touch the various levels of consciousness, but not in a stable way, which would require a real evolution.

In states of consciousness you are able to experience and see things, but then you come out of this state to live your regular life. On the other hand, stages of evolution enable you to always function with a clearer vision of the Way.

Note: Experiences are different from phenomena. An experience will help your training evolve, whereas a phenomenon will divert you from the Way.

3. Transforming the mind

According to the Eight Methods, after transformation comes evolution (see *Secret des Immortels*, French version). This stage of meditation really concerns students practicing full-time: when you start the transformation of the mind, you have already reached happiness (first stage) and revealed your true nature (second stage).

The transformation occurs by "Passing through the Nine Circles of Realization, to go beyond Life and Death." This transformation has a role in the evolution of the mind. In the second stage, the mind had to be clarified and perfected; this implies working on the flaws developed since your birth. In this last stage, the clearing concerns aspects that you have inherited, that you did not develop. It is the process of overcoming any last block that may have lingered on, and going beyond your Pillar of Destiny (Celestial Mandate).

III. The Nine Levels of Realization (in the third stage)

These levels correspond to the three stages (calming, dissociating, uniting) and are watchwords. They enable you to memorize the Way, to know what you are looking for and where you are heading.

The first stage leading to happiness has three levels: watching, occupying, and focusing.

1. Watching

Watching is directly connected to the knowledge you have of your mind. You cannot work on the mind without acknowledging that your mind needs help. Therefore, just watching what you have in your mind is absolutely necessary. You will immediately notice that you have no control over what is going on and that your mind will not respond to your demands. And this is why we need help.

So watching means knowing. We use many different tools to help train this aspect, and you will know better what to choose once you know your mind better. Also, we each have a specific way of operating, and if you are not fully aware of your own particularities, you will not be able to transform the way you are.

2. Occupying, taming

It is said that the mind is like a young agitated monkey. You cannot control it but you can't let it do anything it wants. If you try controlling it by forcing it to calm down, it may work while you are confronting it, but as soon as turn your back it will bite you or run away. Therefore, the only way is to tame it. To do so, you have to spend time discovering it to know it better. Soon you will become friends.

"Occupying" means keeping the mind busy and distracting it in specific ways to gradually tame it without it noticing. This is the part where we use many visualization and counting techniques as distractions from other thoughts. This will gradually make the mind more available. Then it will be possible to access the mind without a struggle.

3. Focusing

Focusing means "using." By this stage you already know more about how your mind works and you must be able to focus your attention for a time on one specific subject; otherwise, it will be impossible for you to train well in Shen Gong. Within the term "focusing" are three further notions: you have to be able to concentrate, focus, and be attentive.

- *Concentrate.* You should be able to set your attention on one object for at least 30 minutes. Your mind is concentrated in a cone-like vision pointing to your object.

- *Focus.* You are in tunnel vision. You stay focused but become aware of what is around you again. You can let "guests" come in—passing thoughts. This is not a problem since you are in an open, focused state and your intention still remains on your initial object.

- *Be attentive, aware.* You still keep your object in mind but you open up and are able to function in life, being aware of everything around you. The completion of this stage is once again what brings you happiness with deep calming.

The stage of Dissociation Aiming at True Realization consists of another three levels: using, holding, and waiting. Here you will be using the Eight Meditations to Conquer Your True Nature.

4. Using

At the end of the first stage your mind is balanced. Now you can *use* your mind in order to make choices to have better perception of the world and yourself. Here, "using" implies being able to really use the various facets of your mind independently.

5. Holding

These are the methods for a balanced mind to come back to equilibrium when you feel you are drifting from your practice. At this point, you can be functioning 80 percent of the time in your daily life with a calmed, balanced mind, but you still have to deal with daily matters, which can cause frictions or tension. This is when it is necessary to have the techniques to return to the center. These are very simple methods, based on positions and connections (the work on the Five Gates too), which bring us back to an alignment. "Holding" also implies being careful in the way we do things to stay in this alignment.

6. Waiting

Although your mind will be clear, something is still missing for complete realization. It just happens in its own time, and this implies waiting. This is the great injustice of the Way. For some, everything will be united and aligned immediately; for others, it takes time, and this part is what we call "waiting." This period of meditation is based on observation. You observe your balance, your stability, and you wait for it all to come together. In this stage there are three main focuses: observe, wander, and be.

The means living your life in balance, through your practice, waiting for the connection to happen. If you complete the dissociation, you become truly accomplished, and this is something that you can very well achieve in your life within society.

The third part, (uniting), however, makes it very complicated to maintain your normal life as you must practice full-time. In this third part of uniting, there are another three levels of realization: observing, connecting, and letting go.

7. Observing

This is the same notion we have above in the process of waiting.

8. Connecting

This is linked to dreams and the work on Guis and the Shens. It is also the link to the invisible world, the link between the instinct and intuition.

9. Letting go

This corresponds to the aimless wandering of the accomplished human being. This ends with the last stage of letting go of life. This is a conscious passing into death.

These are all Nine Levels of Realization.

As students of the Way, our main interests are the Eighteen Methods Leading to the Gates of Madness, because these are exercises that are real tools to help develop our capacities for evolution.

The Eight Meditations to Conquer Your True Nature are also very useful as they will help us become accomplished in our daily life through the clarification of the Human Map within our environment.

The third and last part is really more spiritual and concerns only a minority whose entire lives revolve around the practice. It would be extremely hard to maintain a daily life in society. At this point, very drastic choices have to be made in order to experience this level of Shen Gong.

IV. The Thirty-Five Stages on the Path to the Mind

These 35 stages are composed of:

- The Eighteen Methods Leading to the Gates of Madness (calming the mind)

- The Eight Meditations to Conquer Your True Nature (dissociating)

- The Nine Circles of Realization, to Go Beyond Life and Death (uniting).

The Eighteen Methods Leading to the Gates of Madness

Some of the following methods require a progression (from 1 to 5), but most of them work in synergy and do not have a specific order.

The meditations corresponding to the first stage (calming the mind) are all ritualized; you must take a moment out of your daily life to practice them. In the second stage (dissociating), you find both ritualized meditations and meditations within your daily life. Finally, in the third part of uniting, your life is your practice, and therefore meditation is part of your life.

1. Watch your thoughts

Once again, there is no way you can work on the mind if you do not genuinely observe and come to realize the fact that you need help and that it is necessary to train your mind. The awareness can only come from observation and getting to know your mind.

> *How do you go about it? There is very little to do. You simply take some time to sit doing nothing other than watching your train of thought.*

At first you will experience what we call the "dissipated waiting period." You try to look at your thoughts, but so much is going on that you have a hard time just watching. This adds even more thoughts and you feel you are getting nowhere. After this, another period will be spent feeling there are much better things to do than sitting in this state where nothing happens—just more confusion. This is when your judgment comes in, reminding you that you are not capable and so forth.

Next, you come to a time where these aspects calm down, only for you to experience emotions coming up during this exercise. Often these emotions are inconsistent with what you are living at the time.

Finally, after about six to eight months of practicing this daily, you will notice that it is always the same elements (just like recurrent dreams) that come back during this training. These repeated elements have a particular flavor, and you will know that they concern you directly, even if you do not understand why. These are what trigger the actual work and lead us to the second method.

2. Watch and accept your mind

This means accepting the state your mind is in, the fact that this is the way you are and that is not going to change much, and finally admitting you need help calming your mind. Within this stage there is also a series of phases going from complete denial, negation, to complete acceptance (for instance, the "yes" exercise is part of accepting the way your mind works).

3. Shooting down thoughts (ball-trap)

This is a very active method during which you shoot down each new thought. With an active focus of attention on it, the mind automatically calms down. The more you destroy each rising thought, the longer it takes for a new thought to appear. This can be compared to a child wanting to misbehave while knowing he is being watched!

So the mind is not relaxed here. On the contrary, it provokes a lot of tension, just as a cat backs up when you threaten it, ready to pounce as soon as you turn your back.

With this focused attention, each thought becomes a precise object. You gradually see a string of thoughts just like a string of beads, each thought like a bead, distinct from the others.

The possibility of dissociating one thought from another brings us to an important point. You can only have one thought at a time. You may think that you are thinking of several thing at once, but in fact you are going back and forth between several separate thoughts. There is no such thing as a bag of mixed thoughts. There are only unique thoughts succeeding each other, no matter how fast our train of thought goes. This is very interesting as we discover that our minds can only do *one* thing at a time. Once we see that we only have one thought at a time, it is easier to isolate this thought and look at it as an object.

4. Take a thought and keep it for some time

While you are watching your train of thought, you pick one thought, no matter how insignificant it may seem, and you simply hold on to that thought. For instance, if at some point you are thinking that you forgot to buy bread, then just stick to "buying bread" during your meditation. This exercise can cause tension, but it is a good way to learn how to keep only one thought in mind. Once you are able to do this, you can chase all the other thoughts away.

5. White screen

Now that you can keep one thought, you project it onto the white screen and continue chasing all the others away. You can momentarily feel a true alignment and then the feeling dissipates, just like tuning a radio and almost finding the perfect sound before the crackle resumes. The white screen method is already a small accomplishment. We call it the minor Water and Fire accomplishment.

6. Silence

As we have just seen, finding silence with the white screen method is already a small accomplishment. We call it the minor Water and Fire accomplishment. This is when you find the perfect radio frequency and you are able to stay on it. The alignment is there and you can experience silence. In order to achieve this, you have to go through some steps that cannot be explained without undermining the process you must experience.

7. Working on one sense

The focus can be on one of your five senses—seeing, smelling, tasting, touching, or hearing. You choose one of these five senses and isolate it by placing all your attention on it and focusing on your perception of it. This is an excellent method to soothe the mind while developing your senses.

8. Training the senses

You start by focusing your attention on one sense and then gradually broaden your focus to the other senses, until you reach one full perception of all five senses. What is very interesting is that perception is unique, but it can be activated through several senses at the same time. This training requires a very specific protocol, during which we come to realize that the mind only does one thing at a time. This awareness makes the work on the mind easier because you can focus on units rather than a multitude at the same time.

9. Natural counting
This is the act of counting numbers in their natural order. You can have a short or long series of numbers that you repeat.

10. Rhythmic counting
With this method you choose numbers in an unnatural sequence— for instance, 7–3–8. By doing this, numbers stop being numbers and become concepts. This is an excellent way to disturb the mind! This exercise can also be done with your fingers while walking— see if you are able to think of anything else at the same time! These methods artificially empty your mind of thoughts.

11. The fixed image
You project your visual intention on an image and then close your eyes and maintain your focus on the image, keeping it as realistic as possible. You start with a very simple image such as a square or a triangle, then a real object, and then a landscape.

12. Image in motion
You stare at an object for a while and then let it roll on the floor for a few seconds and focus on its direction and motion. Close your eyes, keeping this in mind. Your attention is on the memory of the object in motion. This is a very dynamic meditation because when the mind develops a thought with a motion, it triggers a real movement in the mind. We call this the Valley of the Mind's Winds. The visualization of memory in motion activates different areas in the brain.

13. The object-concept

You keep in mind an object or (slightly more difficult) a concept for the entire meditation. It is interesting to pick concepts linked to your own unbalances in the Human Map. You will often get answers after the meditation when you resume your daily life. It is interesting to do this meditation before you go to bed. The concept that was observed for some time will break free and you may find the answers in your dreams.

14. Focus without a concept

Once you are able to keep you attention on one concept, you use the method of observing. This means focusing your attention on the concept but looking at it as you would look at a landscape. Often, and for most people, the same concepts will come up naturally. Usually it starts with sadness, anger, and fear—sadness when you realize that you are afraid, anger in opposition to this fear, and finally just fear! We do not force these notions; we let them arise from our open attention on the concepts.

The following meditations (15, 16, 17, and 18) are methods at the point between the first stage (calming the mind) and second stage (dissociation)

15. Self-attention

This method is directly linked to the unbalances in the Human Map. The focus of attention will be on specific problems relating to your unbalances. This meditation is more ritualized as it requires a specific action similar to winding up a mechanism. Once the meditation is over, you must take some time—go for a walk or sleep—and everything will come out. This method forces the mind to reveal its weaknesses.

16. The world

This meditation is similar to the one above. Instead of directing it towards yourself, however, your focus is on your relationship with your surrounding world—your work, your family, and so on.

17. The ritual of each thing

This is a meditation in action in that you pick a concept that will be your main point of focus all day. If you take the concept of silence, for instance, each action in your day will be defined by this notion. You will pay attention to every detail of your day, making it as silent as possible.

18. The ritual in everything

This is also a meditation in action, although here it is not just a concept that is ritualized throughout the day but involves each and every one of our actions. You pay attention to the way you sit, walk, breathe, eat, speak, the way you hold your pen, and so forth. Everything is done with the practice in mind.

You can better understand why this process is called the Gates of Madness. We are completely divorced from natural spontanaeity and we are developing our true nature (Zin Ran) to find perfection in our daily activities.

The Eight Meditations to Conquer Your True Nature

These eight meditations correspond to the second stage of Shen Gong (dissociating). They are much more linked to Nei Dan and to the body. They are not ritualized since they are practiced within daily life. In the term "true nature" there is the notion of completeness, which implies the Three Treasures: the body, the breath, and the mind.

These eight meditations are directly linked to our personal requirements, and therefore we will practice them according to our unbalances. The first four meditations balance the Shen. The second four meditations are connected to four animals.

1. The Path of Truth

This is a meditation to clarify the mind and make it more available. It triggers physical sensations since there is work on breath. In the Path of Truth, we are supposed to dissolve the false to let the truth emerge. We are going to use the "Sword of Knowledge" to cut through obstacles on this Path.

2. The Path of Knowledge

This is a meditation linked to breath and posture, which enables us to clear things and make space. This method is a way to forget the useless things and to store the more useful things—just as you would make space for a new piece of furniture in your living room by getting rid of undesired objects first. The meditation involves the body, the structure, and the breath, but all are directed towards Shen Gong.

> *Matteo Ricci (1552–1610) was an Italian priest who went to China and studied Chinese civilization. He established a way to memorize things, which he called the Palaces of the Mind. He based his technique on ancient Daoist and Buddhist methods, which made space in the mind in order to take in more knowledge.*

3. The Path of the Warrior

Here you will tackle the mind and its troubles by fighting it as a warrior fights the enemy in war. This is therefore a very dynamic meditation!

There will be many techniques involving the "ball trap" method, but this is applied not only to the mind. It will overflow into your life, using that same caution in each of your actions. Each second of the day will be controlled by this military discipline in order to clarify the mind. You take in each new situation and treat one after the other. This system is very dynamic but also more restrictive on the Shen Gong level. You need to plan this meditation and apply it to one situation, and then you will have to catch your breath before resuming another day!

4. The Path of Abandonment

This is the opposite of the Warrior's Path. Here, the meditation is a mix between perceiving and letting go, with the idea of acceptance. There is a reminder of these notions in the morning, and then you carry on with these in mind throughout the rest of the day. This meditation is much more flexible because everything is considered right. It is therefore much more agreeable too!

It is important to have moments in the practice where you let go, especially after difficult meditations during which each second is spent correcting yourself.

Following are the final four meditations, each linked to an animal. There are six animals altogether, four of which we learn about here.

- *The Black Turtle*, or the "mysterious warrior," corresponds to the water element and is linked to the Kidney, the will to stay alive, and your defense mechanism. It is the strength and ability to focus. It also corresponds to the union of the Three Treasures. Finally, it is a link to the lineage as the Path goes through the Black Turtle.

- *The White Tiger* corresponds to the metal element and to the Lung, and also to martial arts, war, and aggressiveness. It is the instinctive strength and the ability to use violence wisely. It is the explosive cry you let out in the Fa Jing.

- *The Green Dragon*, or the "luminous sorcerer," corresponds to the Wood element and to the Liver, to recognition and knowledge, intuition, true creativity (not through imagination but more linked to genius), and everything linked to dreams, contact with the other world, Guis and Shens, and Daoist magic.

- *The Red Phoenix* is also described as a character who is "neither dead nor alive." It corresponds to the Fire element and the Heart—true power. It is said that the Red Phoenix enables us to die and be reborn in order to be connected between two worlds. It is our spiritual side.

5. The Path of Silence

This is a meditation on the Red Phoenix. We expand our ability to be thankful and happy for all that we have and stop complaining about what we do not have. There is an entire process to reverse the way we comment on our life. Here, instead of constantly pointing out what we are missing, we spend our time seeing what is going well for us. This complete change is what we see as being reborn.

6. The Path towards Peace

This seems like a very soothing meditation, but in fact it is a meditation on the White Tiger and it is far from peaceful! Like the Warrior's Path, this is a meditation that you cannot do in just one day. You need about five days to prepare and the meditation; you can also be quite shaken afterwards.

7. The Path to Freedom

The work here is mainly on the connection to our perception of the invisible, of signs and life. It is also a meditation on the development of our intuition. This meditation is really linked to the instinctive part of us, but it develops our intuitive part (it will be the other way around in the following meditation). The work is directly linked to the Po. You work the Po to develop the Hun through the meditation of the Black Turtle. It is the Zhi aspect that will give the impulse and determination to work on the Hun–Po vertical axes in the Human Map.

8. The Path to the Origin (Yuan)

This is the meditation linked to the Green Dragon. It is the opposite of the previous meditation because here we use our intuition to develop our instinct. We work the Hun to develop the Po. These methods are very useful because we cannot confront the Hun or the Po directly; we need the opposite to access and work on each one.

These eight meditations do not necessarily follow each other. They work in synergy. They offer a series of tools such as "the sword of knowledge," or the attention to your daily life, to the way you do things. All these add up and each works on one aspect of your life. There are some that you will not have to use because you already master some aspects of your life, while others will be very useful.

Despite their coherence, it is very difficult to maintain balance between all the aspects of the Human Map. When you train one of them, the others are not stabilized on the same level of focus. For instance, when you train your Nei Dan, your Shen Gong is not necessarily as acute, in that you may have thoughts running through your mind at the same time, and vice versa.

> *This is the problem in achieving your realization. Every aspect that has been worked on and clarified must then find its place in a global unity.*

The body of tools in the Eight Meditations gives a structure, which supports the entire process of dissociation and unification, hence allowing a true realization. Then comes the moment when you have done everything you can and just have to wait for the realization to happen. Nevertheless, despite all the work done to unify all the aspects of the Human Map, sometimes it happens and sometimes it does not. This can be compared to medicine. In reality, medicine does not cure; it just reinitializes the body, either with very energetic or mystical methods such as Tibetan or Daoist medicine or through more structured invasive medicine such as surgery. In any case, after the treatment the body is back to zero. Some people can heal immediately, for others it can take more time, and some never heal. Everything possible has been done to help the patient, but then you just have to wait and see if it works.

In the process of realization you find the same concept. In each person's destiny there are several things that determine your life: the Pillar of Destiny, luck—and everything else! So there is a really unfair component in whether or not you become accomplished in the second part of Shen Gong. Sometimes being unlucky will help to fulfill your destiny because it can force you to overcome your boundaries and lead you, after much effort, to your realization. But it will have been a much harder and longer process than for other people.

The only way to overcome these destiny factors, such as bad luck or your heritage, is in the third part of Shen Gong when you "Go beyond Life and Death." At this stage you will go find the source of your problem. However, if the realization never comes, there is no way to continue on to the third part of Shen Gong, since in the third part you must already be centered, all the elements being united.

Nevertheless, in our school the most important thing is to train the second part of Shen Gong in order to acquire all the qualities of the Human Map. Then, once you have done everything possible and developed all the necessary qualities, experiencing the realization is really secondary. It is the qualities themselves that matter. Indeed, these are the elements that will make our life flow in the best way possible.

The Nine Circles of Realization, to Go beyond Life and Death

We will only give a short overview of these nine meditations as they correspond to the third part of Shen Gong—uniting—and this is only possible after the realization at the end of the second part.

In this last part we are no longer in search of happiness; nor are we in any kind of deep accomplishment of the Way. We are in pure spirituality.

1. Uniting Sky and Earth
This is a precise way to make Daoist magic work.

2. Uniting the Visible and the Invisible
This is a way to use Daoist magic to help appreciate reality and "the other" reality.

3. Uniting Life and Death
This is a way to connect the perception of both worlds with Daoist magic in order to prepare "the second house" when you experience the last passage.

4. Going through the Circle of Dark Lands

5. Going through the Circle of Pure Clouds
The two Circles above are linked to the connection through meditation and seals to Guis and Shens.

6. Accepting the Origin (Yuan)
This is a level of realization that comes by accepting the nature of things (Fire and Water) and the fact that we have to look for the real meaning of life.

7. Returning to the One
This is the idea of stabilizing the magic moments you have experienced through the practice where place and time do not exist. With various techniques you can provoke these moments of unity. This leads to the next meditation.

8. Remaining in the One

This is when these moments with no space and time become stable. To be one is the return to Tai Ji (the union of Yin and Yang).

9. Walking into the Outskirts of Reality

This is the conscious death when you decide or not to go into death as you go to sleep. You go from the Tai Ji to the Wu Ji Hun Dun.

Although we are purely in the spiritual aspect, the structure of these Nine Circles is very interesting. Indeed, the teachings deliver truths with no discussion. Next come the various practices based on these truths. Finally, you will test these truths through the practices.

> *In these Nine Circle meditations there is also an idea of a treasure hunt with clues to find very specific things along the path.*

This is specific to the internal teachings, which are hidden teachings. The information is always dictated as a watchword and sounds a bit strange at first; once you practice, you end up understanding exactly what was meant. The fact that you accept these teachings by following the given path will allow you to purify your Pillar of Destiny and go to your destiny's origin. This is why it is said to "Go beyond Life and Death." Here you are going beyond the reason you were manifested; you are going to its origin (Yuan Shen).

The Guards and the Guests

This is a very important concept in Shen Gong. In your mind there is conscious, provoked activity and some activity that happens on its own.

We compare this to our home. Imagine that you are in your living room. Everything is set the way you mean it to be except that you have people coming through. This is disturbing because you do not want them to come in, but if you try to stop them from entering your space, even more people will intrude.

These are who you call "guests." We do not call them intruders because you are actually responsible for what is happening in your mind! When you are training your Shen Gong, there is a difference between thoughts and guests. Some thoughts arising can be accepted because they are connected to the practice in question. For instance, if one of the meditations requires you to focus on one object—let's say a circle—then you may have some thoughts about the exact shape, color, texture, or clarity of the object. These thoughts are acceptable as they do not divert you from the exercise. On the other hand, if you start thinking about your shopping list or someone you forgot to call, then you are drifting from the meditation, and these are considered guests because they have nothing to do with the practice.

These guests will be accepted for some, but we will also add "guards." Setting up guards is a way to prepare your meditation and decide what the limits will be regarding your guests. For instance, you can decide to let your thoughts come in during some meditations. Before other meditations you can decide to accept only one thought. If another thought rises, stop the meditation and apply the guardian's protocol, in which you have more or less severe methods—sometimes with external tools (sharp objects that will physically remind you!)—to chase the guests and return to the meditation. Despite its spiritual nature, the mind is also part of the body; if you inflict pain, it will prefer to meditate peacefully rather than keep going against the guards!

V. The Eight Steps to Evolution of the Mind

The Eight Steps come from one of the oldest texts of our school and are another way to explain the Thirty-Five Stages. As mentioned, these are "steps" towards an absolute, and you can stop, depending on your limitations, at each step. You can find these steps in all three stages of Shen Gong – training the mind, developing the mind, and transforming the mind.

In the first part of Shen Gong, which leads to happiness, there are five of the Eight Steps:

Step 1: Alertness with thoughts and guests

You sit down, you let your thoughts go—even those that come in as guests, invading your space. Anyone can apply this method: you just watch and let things happen.

Step 2: Alertness with thoughts but no guests

This means you can only accept thoughts concerning the practice, but if you feel it is making you drift from the meditation (any other thought not linked to the practice), then you must stop the thought because it is a guest. This step corresponds to the stage just before the "white screen" in the Thirty-Five Methods.

Step 3: Alertness without thoughts or guests

This corresponds to the white screen method. In other words, you sit down and your meditation is focused on remaining in that moment of nothingness in between thoughts.

Step 4: Attentiveness to an object with no guest

Here, you do not let thoughts come through. You keep one specific object in mind throughout the meditation. You are attentive and not agitated because at this stage you are functioning in the world.

Step 5: Attentiveness with no object or guests

You set your mind in the same way as Step 4 above in order to find one object; in fact, however, you keep no object. You stay on the white screen.

By the end of these five steps, your mind is attentive and available. It is able to stay free from thoughts, and anything is therefore possible now in your Shen Gong training.

In the second stage of developing the mind there are three steps:

Step 6: Attentiveness to nothing with the experience of unity, of light

This is the ability to be united with a unique perception in Shen Gong, when you realize that you have disappeared. You cannot describe this state and it is not conscious, but you realize that a period of time has gone while you were experiencing unity.

Step 7: Attentiveness to nothing with the experience of unity stabilized

Here you are able to stabilize these moments of unity with the capacity of experiencing this state whenever you want. This step corresponds to the practice of the Hun–Po in the Eight Meditations to Conquer Your True Nature.

Step 8: Transformation of the Mind

This corresponds to the third stage of Shen Gong. With this step, you remain in this state of unity naturally. There is no more ritual, practice, or endeavor to experience this. It is just there in your life.

These Eight Steps are very useful to help situate yourself in the practice of Shen Gong.

IV. The Three Impossibilities and Four Dangers
The Three Impossibilities

1. You cannot calm the mind if you disagree with the teachings.

2. You cannot dissociate the mind without the teacher's consent (as he will be the one to give you the methods).

3. You cannot unite the mind without the lineage's agreement (since the unity is linked to the origin—Yuan Shen).

The Four Dangers

1. Dangers of the White Tiger: laziness, distraction, and drowsiness.

2. Dangers of the Black Turtle: ego, importance you give yourself, and beliefs you won't let go.

3. Dangers of the Green Dragon: judgment, prejudice, and habit (linked to your established reflections).

4. Dangers of the Red Phoenix: social life, the mundane, and expectations.

The Four Dangers are linked to four animals, which will each help eliminate the danger in question by training according to that specific animal. For instance, if your problem is drowsiness, you will use an aspect of the White Tiger and go boxing—move!

Dangers linked to the Black Turtle may be more difficult to train, but you can be aware of the flaws and try to correct them gradually.

However, flaws linked to the Green Dragon are extremely hard to tackle because it is your perception that is tainted by your imagination. You think you are doing the right thing when you interpret the training and adapt it to yourself, but in fact you are going astray. This is where the Three Impossibilities have great value to keep you on the right track.

VII. The Three Purities and Nine Chances
This text is dated AD 690.

The Three Purities
The Three Purities are the teacher (the vector), the lineage (the history of the teachings), and the origin (perfection).

The Nine Chances

The Nine Chances comprise the Three Helpers, the Three Chances, and the Nine Misfortunes. The Three Helpers are:

1. *The teacher*, as he delivers the teachings.

2. *The seal*, considered a gift from the teacher to his students to go faster and further than him. The seal provides easier access to profound teachings.

3. *The lineage.* Once you are recognized as a disciple of the Way, you become directly connected to the lineage.

These are the three Pillars of the Way.

The Three Chances are:

1. *The Guardians.* They are in the seal. Their role is the keep the teachings alive and make sure they do not die.

2. *The Shens.* Their equivalent in Western culture is angels; they correspond to intuition, messages, dreams.

3. *The Immortals (Xuan).* There are many levels of possible interpretation. Here these are primarily archetypes and major concepts. Once you understand the story of the Immortals and the symbolism it carries, it can be used as a guide in the Way.

The Three Misfortunes are:

1. *Guis.* These correspond to earthly spirits, like ghosts.

2. *Phenomena.* Often a phenomenon is something you feel during your practice; you then try to reproduce the feeling. Your search for this will trap you into something much smaller than the Way. It is very different from the notion of

experience. The search to reproduce a phenomenon is what will distract you from the Way.

3. *False vision.* By always following phenomena, you gradually create your own mythology. It is the accumulation of various phenomena that gives you a vision, a coherence of the practice, which is false, even if it makes sense to you.

In order to resolve the Three Misfortunes, you need either to have the Three Chances as a balance, or go to the Three Helpers for clarification.

VIII. The Six Advices of the Realized Man

Many of the texts in our school (such as the two Tablets of 100 Characters and small poems), were attributed to Lu Dong Bin, one of the Immortals and founders of the lineage. Sometimes they are presented as "advice from Lu Dong Bin or advice from the Realized Man." Here we will see Six of the Advices attributed to Lu Dong Bin.

1. Understanding the teachings through your practice

You must practice in order to understand what is happening rather than try to understand the teachings intellectually.

2. Balance your practice

In alchemy you need to pay attention and prepare each ingredient with care, and then they can be assembled. The same idea is true when you cook! Each ingredient has its importance and will affect the final taste. The more ingredients you mix, the more important it is to ensure that they are of good quality.

In the practice, human beings have various facets (the breath, the mind, and the body). Each of these facets must be trained in a specific way, with care and understanding, so that when they are united in everyday life, the whole stays coherent and united.

3. Let things happen and listen to the teacher

You let things happen naturally by just following the Way; listening to the teacher will keep you on the Way. Since you never know where you are heading, your entire practice can be tainted with expectations and fantasies. In order to go beyond these beliefs, you must just continue on the Way until you find out for yourself.

4. Follow the Way to not get lost

We are lucky to have a very clear and detailed practice. If you are not sure about an aspect, you must first check the teachings by reading your notes, then check with your fellow students in the school, and finally ask the teacher for clarifications. Otherwise, you could waste time trying to interpret things your own way, thus deviating from the Way! So even if the path in the practice is a longer one, be sure to follow it instead of trying to find shortcuts which might cause you to get lost.

5. Accept the progress in the practice

Each student has his or her own progression in the practice. This is not something that you have control over. You may wish to progress faster, but this will not change a thing. There is a difference between how you would like to evolve in the Way and the reality of what actually happens. This is what has to be accepted by the student. You must let things happen in their own time. The worst thing would be to compare yourself with others and to compare the reality of your progress with your fantasized evolution.

6. Recognize the importance of the Way

This is the idea that you should consider yourself lucky to practice and to have the Way to follow as it gives a guided path, a coherence to your life, and answers and solutions to your problems.

The three other advices are hidden. This completes the first Six Advices, in the same way that the Three Stages complete the Six Levels in traditional Chinese medicine.

Conclusion

Above, we have seen the way Shen Gong is organized. This will allow you to follow the system and situate yourself in the evolution of your practice. It also gives you the chance to choose one method that may suit you best, that you feel more comfortable with, that you enjoy! However, you must practice a while before you know yourself well enough to choose what you like best. The choice is not based on a fantasy but on experience!

You can reach the first stage of Shen Gong—calming the mind—just with one of the Eighteen Methods because they all take the same path and all have the same purpose of calming the mind. By using only one method you will evolve just the same, but you might not necessarily feel it as much as when you adopt several techniques (which also makes the work more dynamic).

> *Two of the qualities that Shen Gong develops are the ability to focus and the ability to be centered. This is crucial to our practice because without these qualities no evolution is really possible in the training.*

Once again, in order to evolve you must practice every day; otherwise, it will not work. There is no "bad" Shen Gong. The fact of sitting down and practicing will be good. It is giving up and quitting that will keep you from evolving. There is no reward if you evolve in your practice. The reward is practicing. It is the journey that is rewarding, not the place of departure and arrival. Besides, if your motivation is driven by a goal, an expectation of some finality, this will always be false. The practice is free of these concepts, as you do not win anything. The steps described in the methods above do not imply a clear linear progression; nevertheless, they all go in the same direction.

What you will notice clearly are some important moments such as:

- When you realize that your vision of life is more positive and you feel good and happy most of the time. This means you have calmed your mind.

- When you realize that your actions are poised, that your movements are not random but a technique applied in life, and that each time you breathe you are doing the Nei Dan. This means you are Realized.

Remember that the mind is perfect because it is immaterial. It is our manifestation of the mind that needs to be worked on in order to reach this existing perfection and to develop the upper spiritual center, which otherwise stays shut down. This is the work of Shen Gong.

Part Six

Deep Nei Dan Practice

Chapter 12

The Way of Nei Dan

This part of the book is a study of the entire inner alchemic system of my tradition. This, of course, implies a life of training, but it is still good to know where you are heading as a student of the Way. Inner alchemy is a part of the Way. It can also be studied on its own. But inner alchemy needs the body and mind for its base. Other schools often need to find exercises from other methods to complete the work of alchemy, thus making it much less efficient. In our school, fortunately, we have had very detailed exercises from the start.

The Way of Nei Dan—inner alchemy—is a way of transformation. There are three main levels:

1. *Foundation.* The foundation is the first and most important level for developing good health and general wellbeing. This is the time in which you establish your practice to stay healthy, have a clearer mind, and make better choices in life. This work on breath is almost sufficient on its own for a great vitality (and crucial for the rest of the training).

2. *Transformation.* Then you have the actual alchemic principle that starts with transformation. It is in fact a principle of dissolution of all obstructions and tensions. This brings out the perfection in each one of us. Although this level may seem complex, anyone who trains can experience this. You

can practice this part easily in one hour a day and maintain a life in society with a family and work and regular hours.

3. *Illumination.* The third level is one of illumination, awakening. It is a way to prepare to die with an attempt to grasp the absolute and return to oneness. In this stage you either chose to stay on earth to teach others or you decide to leave. This is the last principle of internal alchemy.

In order to understand the evolution in Nei Dan, it is very interesting to study the Nei Jing Tu. This is a Daoist diagram of a cross section of a human body illustrated with inner landscapes, poems, and characters, which together explain how to use Nei Dan. Although it does not explain how to start the inner alchemic process, it does give many advanced clues on transformation. There are also many writings about various inner alchemic processes. There is the Chinese Nei Dan, but there is also an Indian and Western alchemic process. The main difference is that the Nei Dan explains what is behind the symbols and the words, and offers us concrete techniques, exercises for each major principle developed. It has very precise explanations of what to do at each level.

In contrast, Western alchemy is much more conceptual, with no explanations or concrete techniques. Indian alchemy focuses on remedies to liberate tensions, with an idea of just letting it happen, but no "manual" on how to go about it!

During Nei Dan work we will see that the given exercises enable us to check and confirm what and where our tensions and obstructions are, and help free ourselves from them in order to continue the stages of transformation. This is done in a very precise way (comparable with the student's diagram of the vertical/horizontal axis structuring the Yi–Zhi/Hun–Po).

So we have very precise tools for Nei Dan. Let's go back to the theory. There are five stages.

First is establishing the foundations with the 300 days of training. In inner alchemy we call this "reinforcing the remedies" or "filling up the supplies." This means making sure you have enough energy when working with inner elements. If you are lacking energy, you will not be able to use what it takes for transformation. So establishing the foundations means reinforcing and pushing the Jing (body), the Qi (energy), and the Shen (the mind). These three major ingredients have to be reinforced, stimulated, and purified so they can become available for the next level's work. This is actually what we do in the basic practice.

If the mind is not calm, if the body is not healthy, and if you lack energy, once you start putting everything in motion it just won't work.

In Nei Dan, when you start moving the breath through the body, at first you may have a strong sensation of the energy circulating, but then it diminishes gradually as you try to move it to certain parts of your body until it just fades away. That's because there is not enough supply! What consumes the most energy of all is the mind: your emotions, judgments, and comments. So if, on the one hand, you try to gain energy by heating the center with specific circulation techniques, but, on the other hand, your mind is preoccupied, your energy will be burnt up before you can even use it properly.

This is why the first step—establishing the foundation—implies developing more energy but also regulating and holding your mind. You can stimulate the energy with very simple yet efficient techniques based on external stimulation to bring Yang energy (self-massage, for instance). There is a Nei Dan inner alchemy but also a Wai Dan, which is the external alchemy with the use of remedies, for instance.

We call the second stage "Transform Essence to gain Qi." This starts with the small circulation in the center of the body (the small celestial circulation with Du Mai and Ren Mai—two of the Extraordinary Vessels, from back to front), which artificially makes us familiar with the sensation of moving energy before it actually happens for real during the transformation of Jing into Qi. By activating the circulation from back to front via these two vessels Du Mai and Ren Mai, the Jing can transform into Qi.

You also need a very good understanding and coordination of the work on breath, along with the sensation of the circulating energy. With the Yi the focus of attention, you can bring energy anywhere in the body. The problem is making the sensation last. Often the energy is depleted fairly quickly. One may have the impression that the more this back-to-front circulation is activated, the less energy there is, as if it were burning out. The other difficulty is the delay when moving the energy from one point to another. It takes time to travel. So the timing has to be precise as well. If you send the energy to a place for too long, since it is Yang it will just leave the body. On the other hand, if you bring the energy to a place but forward it to another place too quickly, nothing will happen either.

Energy that is not guided by intention will just go away. So the precise timing consists in bringing in the energy, following it, and sending it to a specific place before it dissolves. By doing this circulation regularly, the timing is familiar and leads to a rhythm that becomes a dynamo system creating energy. This will clearly feel this with possible sensations of heat, vibrations, a shaking of the body and so on. It is said that it takes about 100 days to reach this stage.

It is only at this point that you can access the third stage— transforming the Qi into Shen (the mind). Once you have gained the energy that brings vitality and health, and you are aware that the system works and is good for your body, you will need to open your energy system to the outside.

The circulation you have developed remains solely your own energy circulation. So it is never perfect because it is charged with all of your problems (remember that you keep on living in society and have to deal with daily matters). These can be seen as the waste that polluted your perfect energy. In order to free yourself from this waste, you just have to put the internal circulation into relation with the outside. This is exactly what we do with breathing—inhaling and exhaling. The exchange between the inside and outside is crucial for our survival.

So why transform the Qi into Shen? Mainly because, thanks to this circulation, you enhance your connection to what is called the Five Gates, as well as your connection to nature, to your partner, and to the outside world in general. This connection to the outside will bring a much more Yang energy, and therefore a better connection to Yuan Qi. This corresponds to the Great Circulation. It takes about a year to reach this stage.

The fourth stage is transforming the mind to return to Dao (nothingness). This stage is clearly a spiritual one where clear choices and renunciations have to be made. One can no longer lead a regular life in society. At this stage you are out of the regular practice and halfway towards giving up life to return to nothingness. This stage takes about three years and requires making choices and major changes, discriminating, and filtering in order to keep practicing.

Nevertheless, it can still be done if everything is organized towards making the practice the priority in life.

This level is linked to a stage called the Golden Path, a meditation on Chong Mai. This vertical vessel goes through our body and is not physically limited to our body. The Dao De Jing speaks of the world's Chong Mai alignment on the human's Chong Mai. This is represented by Man being between Sky and Earth. The "Golden Way" is a work on enlightenment, God, and Dao. As far as the term "nothingness" is concerned, we prefer to see it as space and possibility—availability. Who wants to go into nothingness! Here, the idea is that there is, on the contrary, everything—an absolute.

On the same note, the practice does not change you to make you a better person; it enables you to express more accurately what is good within. This is called Zin Ran. It is the natural part of you, freed and expressed.

The fifth stage is remaining in the Dao to crush the Dao (returning to the non-manifested chaos). This last stage corresponds to monastic practice, far from daily life in society. This is a nine-year period in search of enlightenment and to reach the last human levels of evolution before going back and teaching. This stage is purely spiritual and there are practically no more daily actions.

Now that we have presented an overview of inner alchemy, we can go deeper into each stage, with more detailed information and also ways to experiment in every part of Nei Dan. The experiments consist in searching for sensations, and in that respect they are done artificially, as opposed to the alchemic process during which the sensation must come to you naturally. The good side of doing these experiments artificially is that they prepare the body and unblock it, making it ready for the natural work to happen during the alchemic process.

Questions
What is the difference between Shen Gong and Nei Dan?

In Shen Gong, the focus is more on stillness, with a capacity to block out the outside world for a time to return to oneness. This helps to connect more easily to Yuan Shen. It stimulates the energy and the Shen, but this practice does not apply to daily life's reality. You have to come back to reality after the work. It is purely mental work with no specific breath or body techniques (which have been acquired earlier on). So Shen Gong is really a regulation of emotions and a simplification of the vertical/horizontal axis—Hun–Po/Yi–Zhi).

It is contemplation of how our mind works. In Shen Gong work, the return to oneness goes through dream work and spiritual journeys and also by the purification and transformation of emotions in energy. The main goal in Nei Dan work is to enable the Yin to become more subtle, more refined, by bringing a lot more energy into the body and by regulating all its functions. Our body will undergo concrete changes: the skin, muscles, and tendons change. As the entire system is more efficient with a refined Yin, this will bring in more Yang energy. This increase in Yang will purify the Yin, and the purified Yin will bring more Yang and so on. By purifying the Yin–Yang system, we try to reach the Yuan Qi, Yuan Shen.

What is Nei Gong?

The Nei Gong is work in which we simplify the Wai Gong work (the body work). The body's memory absorbs this work through each tendon and muscle, and it then starts to be rooted so deeply that it becomes very natural. Our mind no longer tries to remember or correct the movements. The mind is then free to concentrate solely on sensation.

Where do we situate the Nei Dan work within the three levels of work: body, mind, and energy?

At a certain point the work on body, mind, and energy becomes more complex; each has many facets and details. But we don't take in everything at once. During our evolution in the practice we always use an aspect, exercise, or technique that suits us best. When you evolve in Nei Dan work, you also evolve in the three levels of training. Everything is linked and evolves naturally.

The main reason each part is separated is that too much information at once "kills" the practice. This is particularly true in the Western world, where, instead of training each aspect thoroughly, we assume that knowing about something in theory gives the same results as practicing! But if you don't take time to practice, it just will not work.

Furthermore, if you start training with too much information, you have a tendency to go from one thing to another much too quickly... And nothing happens! Instead, you should focus on one thing at a time in order to root it deeply in your body and mind so that it becomes natural.

This is why in our school each aspect of the practice is clearly separated. By excelling in one, you can improve all the others because they are linked.

This is also why there are so many techniques for each aspect of the practice. This enables the student to find one that works best for him, even in one of the training aspects he most dislikes! In every part there is always one exercise out of many techniques that will work best for a specific person. Only a disciple or teacher of the Way has to know all the exercises possible! For the regular student, two or three exercises in each aspect of the Way will be sufficient to evolve. The practice is already very complex and demanding. There is no reason to add more difficulty by using techniques or exercises that don't work for you.

I. The foundations

This is what will be the most useful for many of us. The main ingredients in order to work on inner alchemy are Jing (essence), Qi (energy), and Shen (mind).

Jing

As we discussed at the beginning of this book, the Jing represents the incarnated, materialized body, but it can also be compared to a little meter with numbers rolling down and decreasing daily. How much Jing you have will depend on what was passed on to you by your parents and lineage; the Jing can vary from person to person. Unfortunately, we are not equal in terms of the amount of Jing we start out with! We all start with very different potentials.

So the idea is simple. There are three points of focus:

1. The body has to work well before anything else, and for this you have to reinforce it, ground it, and relax it.

2. You also have to think of your Jing capital and how to avoid depleting it.

3. In order to preserve your Jing, there are ways to gain more Jing.

There is a difference between innate Jing (what you were born with) and acquired Jing. You build your acquired Jing by eating and breathing. So it is something you can control, unlike innate Jing. The goal is to understand the best way to gain this energy in order to build a solid foundation for your body and mind, and to preserve your essence.

Qi

Qi is mainly acquired through movements. The focus of attention is on the sensation of each movement, and this transforms Wai Gong (external practice) into Nei Gong (internal practice).

What is important is to understand how each position and movement in the Nei Gong work has a different effect depending on whether it is large, small, fast, slow, and so on. Also, you will choose the most appropriate one to gain maximum energy according to your health and needs. Body work is the easiest in the sense that each movement can be corrected by the teacher and eventually you will get it right.

Work on the breath is already harder because you can be overwhelmed by emotions. These emotions have an influence on the quality of the breathing exercise, and this is something that cannot be corrected from the outside.

Shen

The same is true for mind work. It is very hard to find your mind going in all different directions when you are looking for stillness!

This is why, at this level, you have a method you can follow! For mind work you first have to see how the mind operates so that you can tame it and then separate the three minds—who you think you are, who you pretend to be, and who you really are— only to then reunite all of the facets through Shen Gong work. This is very simple Shen Gong since we are still establishing the foundations and looking for an available mind.

When can you tell you have established the foundations? There are three basic factors:

1. You have good coordination
This implies that you are able to repeat a new exercise within ther next ten minutes of seeing it for the first time (within the limits of your body's capacities, of course!). Coordination is the ability to see, understand, and repeat a movement. This requires a relaxed body and mind. If you try to work on Nei Dan without good coordination, the blocks will remain in the body and keep you from achieving the Nei Dan work. And if you try to unblock the tensions and obstructions only through Nei Dan, it will take many more years. This is why exercises to unblock your body and improve coordination are crucial.

2. You have a strong body
After six months of training you will feel stronger than before you started. If you do not see your strength develop, it can only be because you are not doing the movements properly or you missed some elements of the practice. In this case you can ask your teacher for more details and corrections.

3. You are grounded
You must be physically grounded (not just in feeling). When you are grounded, the body is able to hold the mind. This makes the first exchange Kan/Li (fire and water) much easier—that is, the

exchange between the Jing (the essence) and the Shen (the mind). You cannot do Nei Dan if you are not grounded.

You naturally become more grounded after a few months of practice. You can verify this with all the exercises done with a partner, mainly with pushing and pulling.

In order to set the foundations of Nei Dan, you need coordination and a connection between body and mind to clear the blocks that bring tension. You need to be physically stronger (the training exercises will work the quality of the muscles and tendons). Finally, you must be grounded (with push and pull exercises).

Manage your consumption of energy: Observe your lifestyle

Added to the three aspects above, it is also very important to consider your use of energy—how you consume it in daily life. To discover how much energy you spend daily, you must be aware of your lifestyle and rhythm.

Some basic facts:

- If you don't eat, you have no energy.

- If you eat bad food, you have no energy. Fat, sugar, and dairy products create humidity in the body, and this will block good circulation of energy. Your muscle needs to have a good density; if it is too soft and fatty, this means you have to change the way you eat to eliminate humidity.

- If you don't sleep, you have no energy. You must respect your sleeping cycles according to your needs. The hours before midnight, before the transition from Yin to Yang, are much more beneficial. This is because the reconstruction process during sleep is more Yin. However, oversleeping after midnight is not recommended. This part of the night is more Yang, so if you oversleep when your body and mind should be active, it will be bad for the Yang energy. It is important also to know the number of hours of sleep you need per night. For this you can write down the time you go to sleep and the time you wake up naturally without an alarm clock. If you do this over a period of time (one to two weeks), you will have a better idea of the number of hours' sleep necessary for you. If you are regularly sleeping for fewer hours than you need, this will use up your Jing.

- To maximize the quality of your sleep, you need to go to bed already relaxed. You go to bed to sleep, not to relax. Sleeping allows you to digest the day's events and emotion, and engraves them in your mind. If you do not sleep long enough, this process will not happen and you will not be able to benefit from your daily experience. This is why using relaxation techniques in your practice just before bedtime is crucial.

- It is important to balance your daily activities. Unfortunately, most of us are used to dividing the day between different responsibilities, and the largest part of the day is taken up by work. Ideally, the day should be equally divided between resting time, work, and leisure. Training is considered to be rest as well as sharing time with others. Leisure is mainly doing things that are not useful—just pure distraction.

- Finally, there is also the sexual aspect. This concerns men primarily, because the loss of energy is mainly through ejaculation. Maintaining sexual activity with a partner is absolutely natural and healthy. The only concern would be if you feel tired and empty after sexual intercourse. This should be interpreted as a warning of the need to reduce the frequency of your sexual activity.

Manage your energy

This means understanding your body and working on how to gain more energy and to make it available.

- The spleen/stomach is involved in your good health through a good diet and control of muscle mass and quality.

- The lungs are important not only for their role in breathing exercises, but also to continue breathing well in our daily life. Since this is not natural, you should remind yourself as often as you can to breathe deeply. You will go from a half-liter intake with normal breathing to at least 4 liters when breathing consciously and deeply.

- The liver has an important role in making energy available and keeping it in motion all through the day. If you have to work sitting down all day, you should get up and move a little at least every hour. If you are able to organize your time, the ideal is to do at least ten minutes of exercises for every one and a half hours of sitting. Your body will always be available and it will not build blocks. The sitting position, especially leaning over and typing at a desk is terrible. It blocks the diaphragm, hence your breathing, and the Dai Mai extraordinary vessel (which is circular like a belt). It also block the connection between the Du Mai (back) and Ren Mai vessel (front). This constant position builds stagnation of the liver and can create a lot of frustration.

The foundations and the mind

In order to build the foundations of Nei Dan, your mind has to be available. This requires three elements:

1. Discover and become intimate with the way your mind works
To achieve this, you need to spend time every day observing what is going on in your mind. The way you operate is 90 percent based on habit. So if you go along unconsciously, you can operate through your day without even noticing how your mind works. This is why you need to take some time every day to sit down and do nothing else but focus on your mind and see what thoughts come and go.

What you see—who you see yourself as—is usually very different from what you were expecting You might even ask yourself, "Who *is* this person?" Soon you start to have a better view of how you operate, of your recurrent thoughts, your perceptions, your blocks and judgments.

Another aspect of this introspection can be developed through two very simple and pragmatic exercises:

- Before you go to bed, when you end your day, take a brief moment to look at your day. Recognize and enumerate what bothered you in your actions and thoughts, and what caused frustration.

- The next morning, before you start your day, plan your day, keeping in mind what bothered you the day before. Maybe you can find a better way to go about it this time.

By doing this regularly, you will very quickly and naturally become more conscious of your every action and thought. You will not be able to trick yourself and lie as easily because you know that you will be studying your behavior every night.

2. Sit in complete stillness and watch your mind at work
With this technique you will rediscover stillness and silence.

- Find a very comfortable place to sit and keep the same position the entire time.

- Do not wriggle or scratch yourself if something bothers you. The exercise requires *absolute stillness*. You must even keep your breathing silent!

- The only thing you have to do is watch your mind.

This is not real Shen Gong work, but it prepares your mind and makes it available for future Shen Gong work and for Nei Dan.

3. Sit in complete stillness, watch your mind at work,
and wait for the next thought to come
You start the same way as above. Once you are settled in the exercise, keep your eyes shut and start focusing on the next thought to come. Soon this technique will slow down drastically the profusion of thoughts running through your mind.

These three techniques to train the mind are all you need to set your Nei Dan foundations. They should be practiced daily.

II. Transformation
1. Liberate the Jing to bring the Qi
Nei Dan is the work on energy (Qi). If Yin and Yang and balanced—that is, if the Water below (Jing, the body) and Fire above (Shen, the mind) are stabilized and become balanced—this will liberate Qi (Yin–Yang energy). This new available energy can be used to generate even more energy. In order to liberate the Jing, we have to stimulate the body through Nei Gong work. There are many different ways to train physically. You can use different speeds (slow, fast), various ranges of movement (large or tight), different directions (middle, front, side, back), different positions (centered, one leg behind the other, lying down, sitting, standing), and so on.

Each variation will have a different effect on the way you work your Qi. It is important to know all the possibilities in order to adapt all the techniques according to your needs.

Your position

You can stay in the middle. In the Da Xuan tradition this is the most common position at first. Although it requires being perfectly centered, which takes years of practice, once you find your center you will be working directly on Chong Mai, thus developing the exchange with the outside, the Earth and Sky.

Here is a very useful technique to find your center. Stand straight, feet parallel. Start shifting your weight from your toes to your heels and let the motion create a gentle wave from the bottom to the top of your spine. With the rotation between front and back, you feel your body straightening when you shift to your heels and then back to the weight on your toes, with a tension in the front of the legs. By becoming more aware of the feeling of back and front, you will find your center more easily. This exercise is also very interesting because the rotation of weight on the front and back of your feet makes the Qi, the energy, go down. It soothes and relaxes when you feel tense and irritated.

You can also be positioned one leg in front and the other behind. Your weight can be on the front leg or on the back leg.

When your weight is on the front leg

This means having about 90 percent of your weight on the front leg. This pushes forward and opens the front, which is Yin (the Ren Mai vessel), and it closes and tenses the back, which is Yang (with the Du Mai vessel and Ming Men—DM4), even with the back leg aligned. It projects the energy in front. So the Yang is projected towards the Yin, and this creates a very good balance in energy. Since the Yang nourishes Yin, this position is very useful to generate energy and to stimulate body energy in general. This position also has an effect on Dai Mai (the belt vessel) because the extension of the legs and pressure on the front will stimulate the opening of the Gua and Dai Mai. When you open your Guas, you nourish the upper/lower connection and you push the Yang

Qi (back energy) into Yin Qi (front energy). Since this position will be very stimulating, it is best not to use it for relaxation before bedtime!

When your weight is on the back leg

This means having 90 percent of your weight on your back leg. When your weight is on the back leg, your front foot can either be pointing to the ground or you can be resting on your heel with your toes flexing up. When the front toes point into the ground, you are working on lightness. This position stimulates points such as Feng Long (Stomach 40), Gong Sun (Spleen 4), or Qi Chong (Stomach 30), which all fight humidity in your body. This position makes the Yang circulate. The balance between Du Mai and Ren Mai is improved with this position. If you have trouble with the small circulation when you are working the Nei Dan, you can use this position to boost the circulation and have more sensation.

When your front toes are flexing up and your heel is in the ground, you are working your Tai Yang. This means you are stimulating the whole back part of your body, the Yang, the Bladder meridian, and your defense energy, Wei Qi. This brings a lot of heat and Yang energy. Once again, this is not the best position to use to calm down! If you are more the thin, wiry type, this might not be the best option as you need to have enough Yin (body mass) to hold the Yang.

You can work very low on your knees. If you are under 15 years old you can work in a very low position! Otherwise, training very low can hurt your joints. Nevertheless, after training for a while, when you feel comfortable with some techniques, you may feel the need to go down lower on your knees on some movements. It is good to go ahead and try this, but it must always feel comfortable and not painful. It must feel natural. This happens at a stage where the body has gained and transformed a lot of energy into Yin, and your muscles and tendons become stronger. Working on a lower level makes the energy go down as well, and this specific low position will enable you to keep the energy. This position also soothes the mind.

Standing up

Traditionally, it is said that when you work standing up, you reinforce the Great Circulation, the exchanges with the outside.

Sitting down

When you train sitting down, you work the Small Circulation.

Lying down

When you train lying down, you work everything related to Shen Gong, the mind and the emotions. Practicing movements lying down may not be favorable to energetic exchanges in the way they usually are in a standing position. However, on a difficult day, emotionally or mentally, it will enable you to soothe the mind and make your mind more focused and available for the rest of the training.

Training at different rhythms

In order to consciously choose a rhythm during your practice, you have to first be aware of your position, of how you stand (the exercise of "conscious walking" is excellent to feel yourself in space). When you become aware of yourself in space, you can more easily judge the exactitude of your movements and also their speed.

Fast movements

Fast does not mean accelerating from time to time or going a bit faster and then the normal way. Fast means going as fast as possible during the entire exercise. This is very hard to do because more often than not you lose the structure of your movement at the same time. Fast movements will help clarify your intellect, intention, and your will and capacity to take action (Yi–Zhi axis).

It implies going faster in your mental process in order to achieve speed in movement.

Slow movements

As with fast movements above, slow does not mean slowing down a bit or decelerating from time to time. Slow means going as slowly as possible and slowing down the movement even more at each millimeter in space! Slow movements help the development and balance of your Hun–Po vertical axis. This is the balance between your intuition, pure mental form, and connection to spirituality above and the instinctive, pure physical, and proprioception below.

Fa Jing: Explosive force

This is a rather slow movement, which prepares for an explosive movement.

The Fa Jing gathers all the elements required above (Yi–Zhi, Hun–Po). What comes out of this explosiveness can be likened to a kick in your Jing. And it actually is a kick in the secret root of your Jing. This represents your hidden potential. And you must do the necessary work to awaken and reveal it. Each time you do Fa Jings, you work on making this potential more accessible.

> *Often, though, you can hurt yourself with Fa Jing exercises, partly due to their explosive nature but also because when you come closer to the truth too quickly without being prepared, it hurts!*

Fa Jing requires a lot of energy. If you feel you are lacking energy, it is best to just do one rather than repeat a series. When you train at Fa Jing, you experience great moments of clarity just after the exercise.

Three qualities to reinforce the body
Feeling
The Spleen and Stomach meridians control flesh and muscles. In order to stimulate them, you have to feel your body in motion. When you are focused on the sensation of your movement, on the tendons and muscles, you will reinforce them much faster than if your mind is not attentive. This is based on Chinese traditional medicine as well as Daoist medicine. So if you are focused on the sensation of your movement during training, you will also be reinforcing the Stomach and Spleen meridians.

Absorb and project
First and foremost, to train "absorb and project" (push and pull) you have to focus on being grounded and centered during the entire movement. This is a good way to develop these qualities. You also work on the limits of your body, the exactness of each move, and particularly the precision of the upper body movements in connection with the lower body being grounded. Absorb and project exercises work on the essence of enthusiasm and defensive energy.

Grabbing
In the grabbing exercises you work the connection between all the muscles and tendons from your fingers down to your toes. By training these connections, the multitude of tendons and muscles become one. The movement is controlled by one tendon going through the body. The work is on the Jue Yin and the Shao Yang, which correspond to the Liver energy and the regulation of the upper, middle, and lower functions of the body (breathe, assimilate, and secrete). These meridians control the fluidity of the circulation throughout the body. By creating one link throughout the body, the energy flows more easily, just like opening an energy highway through the body rather than taking all the small back roads.

The three techniques above can be applied to any Qi Kung movement.

Training the various directions

First, there are the main direction lines: up, down, right, left, front, back. When you work on these lines, you are training the Yang level in your body.

Up/down

The up and down arm movement is linked to Chong Mai and stimulates the Tai Yang level. It is a work on balancing the Water (below) and Fire (above) in our system, what is deepest to what is most superficial, the Jong Qi (ancestral energy) to Wei Qi (defensive energy). Training the up/down movement is what will bring the most energy, especially when you add to this the work on sensation, absorbing and projecting, and grabbing. Here you have access to a complete training! The only trouble with these simple movements is the capacity to stay focused long enough and not get distracted too easily. Furthermore, there are so many other techniques available, it would be a shame not to explore them!

Right/left

The right/left arm movement means going from the center to each side (45 degrees from the center) and back. The work on right/left stimulates the Shao Yang level (Liver and the Triple Energizer) and Dai Mai (the belt vessel), responsible for a good connection between the upper and lower body.

Front/back

The work on the back and front sensation activates Ren Mai and Du Mai. This work is beneficial for Small Circulation work. It is linked to transformation and this is linked to the Yang Ming level. For instance, if you feel you have to gain weight or, on the other hand, burn excess fat, the front/back movements will stimulate the transformation of food into energy and transform and regulate assimilation. If you understand the qualities above, you can organize your training depending on your needs and adapt every movement accordingly.

By taking in all the various aspects of training above, you take away the chance factor, hoping that something will eventually work, and really become aware of the direction you are taking and how it is up to you to make it work.

Training circles
Working on a frontal plane will stimulate the Tai Yang. Working on a sagittal plane will stimulate the Yang Ming/Tai Yin (with the work on front/back, the Ren Mai/Du Mai). Working on a horizontal plane will stimulate the Shao Yang (Triple Energizer) and Jue Yin (Fire).

The range of motion
If you take the center of your chest as one line and your shoulders as another line, you are at a 90-degree angle. Usually you work within a range of 45 degrees, which means imagining a line in the middle of the 90-degree center-to-shoulder angle. As long as you work within this range, you will be able to work to balance the energy with the gentle stimulation of Tai Yang, your Wei Qi.

You can change the range in which you train for specific reasons. You can expand your movements away from the center as though stretching your arms out on each side. You will feel torsion in your center as if a belt on your stomach was twisting one way and the other. This is the work of Shao Yang and Yang Ming (Stomach and Large Intestine). As a result, you will be stimulating the transformation of food and its proper assimilation.

On the other hand, you can make the range smaller than the regular 45-degree angle by dividing it in two. This corresponds to a line starting from the nipple. So when you are working a smaller than usual range of motion, the range goes from the center of your chest to your nipple. All the movements will be trapped within that zone.

Furthermore, on a vertical level you will not go past Tian Tu (which is situated on Ren Mai—CV22—in the dent at the base of the neck in the center of the collar bone) on the top and Qi Hai on the bottom (CV6—about an inch and a half under the navel). The movements will be condensed and limited to a minimum range of motion. This puts the energy under pressure, and you will feel this too, just like a pressure cooker! This works on the Jue Yin and Shao Yang (Liver and Triple Energizer). It brings a lot of heat and you may even start sweating after the exercise. This is due to the rise of energy at the end of the exercise.

Working within this small range is ideal to decongest stagnations and make energy flow more fluidly. It is also very beneficial when you are ill because it cleans the entire body from stagnation.

> *Note: In all these various techniques you always want to make sure that you combine rhythm, direction, and range of motion in a reasonable way. If you feel tension and muscular soreness in a relatively large area (such as the entire shoulder), you can keep practicing, but it would be wise to slow down the rhythm, for instance, if you are using wide-ranging motions, or readjust your movements. If you happen to feel sharp pain in any position, you must stop immediately as this means you are doing something wrong and will hurt yourself.*

In this chapter we have detailed the techniques to use in order to gather the maximum of ingredients to purify the Jing (the body), the Shen (the mind), and the Qi (the energy), which should enable you to establish the foundations of the Nei Dan work. Not only are we looking for a balance of the body, mind, and Qi, but we are also trying increase all our capacities—more energy overall, with a better mind (more available), better breath, and a stronger body.

If you gain a lot of energy, it will avoid tapping into your Jing as you will always keep a protective cushion on the energy available for daily use.

If you have a weak Jing, it is just like having $2 in your checking account. It is not a problem to just have $2, but you can't spend it! If you earn a lot regularly, you will never have to withdraw that $2 and you will keep your account.

You can start the Nei Dan work at any time. As far as age is concerned, the main difference is that when you are very young your mind will have a harder time being available, and when you are older you will have to work a longer time on all the blocks that have accumulated over decades. From the age of 30 the aging process starts. Our practice will improve all qualities on a mental, physical, and energetic level. Therefore, there will be a balance between the ascending training process and the natural aging process. This is what we call "Daoist immortality."

And if you think you are over-training, remember this. You can never have too calm and available a mind, your breath can never be too extensive, and you can never have too much energy and too strong a body!

2. Transforming the Jing into Qi

Here we are going one step further in the transformation. The term that defines this stage is "Using the Jing to transform it into Qi." The foundations are based on the balance between fire (Heart) and water (Kidney), a centered essence and mind. It is the balance of these two ingredients that will enable the transformation of Qi. So the role of the Jing and the Shen is to make the Qi come out. Here, transforming the Jing into Qi means using the potential essence to make Qi. Using the foundations' three ingredients as a base, the Yin and the Yang reveal the Yin/Yang.

This stage requires 100 days of training. This means that it is a short period (about a third of the time required to establish the foundations). It corresponds to a moment when you put things into motion. You will not be able to experiment at this stage without the foundations. You need to have trained each aspect of the foundations first. When this is achieved, the next step is going to be physical work to awaken, stimulate, and make available the energy you've accumulated.

There are two methods for this.

1. The long way: circular massage around the navel for 45 minutes. Using your fingers, you massage firmly in circular motions around the navel, going from the center, out to about 2.5 inches, and back to the center again. So that the skin doesn't get irritated, you can use a piece of silk.

2. The short way: percussion under the navel. Slightly cup your hands and drum firmly in the same area approximately 2 inches under your navel. The width of your hand fits perfectly in the space just above your pelvic bone (between Qi Hai and Guan Yuan). The rhythm should correspond to about four percussions a second and the impact should be strong enough to produce a sound. The exercise should last 15 minutes. Students already intensively training by the "Iron Shirt" (using percussion on your body to thicken fascia and make it stronger) need more pressure; instead of cupping the hands, the index knuckles are used like a nail being hammered.

Once the process above has been completed (the foundations acquired and the above exercises executed), we have to light the Three Fires in order to release pure energy. The Three Fires are:

The center

Heating the center is preparing the mass of energy that you are going to work with. The hands are placed under the navel. When you inhale, you become aware of your center, and when you exhale, you increase its sensation. Increase the sensation when you exhale throughout the entire process.

> *Note: Heating the center does not necessarily mean that you feel heat in the zone. The sensations can differ. You can feel tingling, numbness, or even cold, for instance. Once you train the center, the sensation goes from superficial to deep, with a feeling of density.*

The points

Once the sensation of the center is developed, you will practice feeling points on a trajectory. The exercise consists in changing your focus of attention from the center to the surface, and moving the sensation of energy from one point to another. The main points are on the central line of your body from front to back.

Start from the center down to Qi Hai, the perineum, and then back up to Ming Men, the kidneys, and between the shoulder blades. Then you keep moving the sensation up to Dai Zhui or the base of the occiput. Make sure not to stop in between these two points because this part of the neck tenses up quickly. Finally, you move the sensation to Bai Hui, the top center of the head, and then down again to the front of the body. The main points in front will be the third eye, Tiantu (at the base of your neck in the dent before your collar bone), then to the center of the chest (emotional center), and finally back down to the center and navel. These are the main points on this circular path. To bring the sensation to a point from the center, you must start focusing on the point when you inhale and increase the sensation at the point when you exhale. You will no longer feel the sensation in the center. When you inhale again, you check that you are on the right point, and with the exhaling you intensify the feeling again. Once your feeling of the point is clear, you can move on to the next point on an inhalation. You then repeat the same process on each point.

> *Note: When you are moving from one point to another, you do not want to push the energy towards the following point. Just proceed as above and focus on each point, one after the other. Otherwise, the energy will dissolve.*

At first the sensation of energy has a tendency to fade fairly quickly and there is usually not enough to go through all the points. This is why initially you want to reduce the circulation to the lower level—from the navel to Qi Hai, the perineum, and Ming Men, then back to the center and navel again. This is the small circulation circle. Once you are able to maintain the energy on this small level, you can widen the circle by going up between the shoulder blades and back to the front in the center of the chest and down again.

Finally, when you are ready, you can use all the points.

The Little Orbit

The Little Orbit is a spontaneous rise of energy that can be experienced once you have practiced the work on points and mastered the artificial circulation. First, start by heating your center well. Then, by using your perineal muscles on an inhalation, pull up the energy from your center to your back. The energy should rise naturally up your back until it passes back to the front at the top of the superior palate. Then you swallow (just on the first cycle) and the energy naturally goes back down to the center when you exhale.

The pace of the rising energy is not very fast. It takes about six seconds from bottom to top. It is not sudden! This is why the work on breath is so important. You need to inhale long enough for the energy to take the time to rise; otherwise, if you exhale too soon, the Yang energy will fade before rising to the palate. If you are able to maintain your inhalation until that point, the Yang will pass into Yin, and the descent of Yin is much easier as it simply follows the exhaling. On the other hand, if your inhalation lasts too long—that is, if you are still inhaling when the energy has past Bai Hui—then the energy will dissipate as well. The timing is crucial. It is very important to synchronize the breathing with the rise of energy. The inhalation has to follow the pace of the rising energy. You must find the rhythm for the exhalation as well.

The great Secret of Nei Dan is that you have to finish inhaling when the energy comes to Bai Hui. And you must start to exhale while finishing the Du Mai (between Bai Hui and the upper palate). Then Du Mai and Ren Mai connect by the tip of the tongue touching the upper palate.

If you have trained the breath well, in addition to all the aspects of the foundations, both the energy and the breath should synchronize naturally. If the energy does not rise further than your kidneys, this means you need to work on the points more and also on your breathing.

> When you are working on the Little Orbit, you may wonder if what you are feeling is truly energy. The previous work on the points should answer your questions since you will know by then the difference between an imagined sensation and the true sensation of energy on a point. This is why it is crucial to follow each step thoroughly. It is good to practice this circulation for at least 30–45 minutes.

Here we are not yet in the deepest transformation of the Nei Dan work, but we are at a stage of transformation that will bring most vitality.

3. Transforming the Qi to nourish the mind

In the second part above we have seen how the Jing and the Shen enable the Qi to reveal itself. In this small circulation work, you need to keep an alignment during the exercise. The mind and the body are raw material here, used as ingredients in the transformation process. If you are distracted during the exercise and lose your focus and intention, you will instantly dissipate the Qi. Consequently, you will have to resume the exercise from the start. Having an available mind does not mean having no thoughts at all during the work; it implies not being bothered by your thoughts and keeping your attention on the sensation.

When you are able to stay focused, the manifested Qi gradually becomes more pure and refined, progressing in each cycle of the circulation work. As a result, this refined Qi will purify the Yin and clarify the Jing–Shen connection (body–mind). The more you practice, the more refined the Qi will become. When you practice sufficiently, the Little Orbit circulation will flow smoothly.

Giving birth to a spiritual embryo: Ling Tai
At this point, when your mind and body are calm and available during the Nei Dan work, you naturally enter the third level of the transformation. Now the only raw material you need is your breath, your Qi. You then start a ten-month process called "Giving birth to a spiritual embryo." Ten months correspond to the gestation time in traditional Chinese and Daoist medicine. When the breath work becomes more pure, it rises. This means that your feeling of the center becomes denser and rises from under the navel to the stomach or chest. This is due to the purified Qi, Ling Tai, becoming more Yang, thus rising. It is so Yang that it can no longer stay in the lower level of the body. The "spiritual embryo" can be born after this ten-month gestation period. In the Nei Jing Tu, this birth is represented by a pearl rising from the top of the head.

The small realization of Kan and Li
This is the moment when the Heart and the Kidney (Jing and Shen) become perfectly balanced. This stage is expressed through

the liberation of many hidden emotions as the spiritual embryo rises to express itself. This is a fairly unpleasant moment and it can last quite a while.

Working the Small Circulation with the sensation on the lower center brings a feeling of wellbeing. On the other hand, the sensation of the center rising to the chest (the center of emotions) is quite disagreeable and you can feel overwhelmed by hidden emotions gushing out. When you feel this happening, however, this also means it is time to move on to the next stage.

Flooding the Five Gates: The Great Circulation
This is the process of nourishing the Five Gates. This is no longer a circulation contained within your body limits between Kan and Li, the Jing and the Shen. We are in a larger circulation of energy between yourself (the inside) and the world (the outside). This changes the sensation as well. The sensation of energy is no longer on the Small Circulation. The energy is now drawn to the limit of your body, first on the Wei Qi (defensive energy), then on the Five Gates. At this point, it will be necessary to train the Xin Yi Dao Yin Fa (emotional work) in order to calm your mind, especially your emotions, due to the difficult transition with the Kan/Li process. This specific training on emotions will free the energy blocked in the different organs and will make it available for this level of Nei Dan work. If you do not have this tool, it will be extremely difficult and you can stay blocked in the smaller circulation with emotions gushing out every time.

> *This is a stage at which you need your mind to focus on the Five Gates without being disturbed by your intense emotions. The two together are not manageable. Therefore, you must train the Xin Yi Dao Yin Fa at this stage of the alchemic process.*

As soon as the emotions are soothed, you can start the work on the Great Circulation, letting the energy come in and letting the energy go out of your body. By exchanging with the outside, your Qi will be increasingly purified.

How do we train the Great Circulation?

Traditionally, the Great Circulation is practiced outside in nature, exchanging with all the elements (water, trees, etc.), but also it can be shared with a group or another person (sexual alchemy). In the more esoteric aspect of Nei Dan, the exchange is with the stars and the sky. In order to train the Great Circulation, you start with your center as in the Little Orbit circulation, but instead of creating an inner cycle from back to front, you are going to bring the energy to your hands and to your feet. In this way you take the energy as far as you can from yourself. First, you place your hands on your thighs or raise one hand in front of you, palm open and facing out. Then you start the same work of sensation as in the Small Circulation. Only the places where you focus your attention change. Inhale and feel your center; exhale and feel the energy in your hand. As you repeat this breathing, you will increasingly feel the coolness of the air entering your palm when you inhale and the heat coming out of your hand when you exhale.

If you are uncertain about the difference in sensation, the following technique will help. Inhale through your mouth with a "hen" sound. This will cool down your hand as you are bringing the energy in. Exhale through your mouth with an "aaagh" sound. This pushes the sensation of heat through and out of your hand. Normally, the energy will come into the body towards the center when you inhale and go outside of the body when you exhale.

With this in mind, we can start to develop the Five Gates:

- Sit in a comfortable position with your hands free.

- Rest your hands, palms up, on your thighs.

- If it does not create too much tension in your shoulders, raise both hands in front of your chest, palms out, elbows bent.

- If your body is strong enough, open your arms to the side, and point your two fingers (index and middle finger) at a 45-degree angle on each side. This position will give you maximum intention and exchange: first, by doing this you decrease the range of contact with the universe to two fingers; second, by extending your arm tendons, you create a more direct passage for the energy to flow through more smoothly. Consequently, you will have a stronger and clearer sensation.

- In the position above, arms out and two fingers pointed, you can increase the sensation of heat and bring it further out of your body with a rotation. Start with your fingers down when you inhale and turn your arms and fingers up when you exhale. Repeat this with every breathing cycle. Keep the sensation on your center when you inhale and in the fingers when you exhale.

During the entire practice, you must not lose the sensation in your hand or fingers and your center. If you stop feeling one or the other, this means you have lost the connection and you must resume heating the center. You might even have to go back to the small circulation. When you start inhaling and exhaling, exchanging with the outside, you can feel tired and empty fairly quickly. This can be compared to a sponge. In order to really fill a sponge with water, you have to wring it out first before letting it soak up all the water again. If you don't squeeze it firmly, it will not be able to absorb as much water.

It is exactly the same idea with this energy exchange. You feel drained as the Wei Qi leaves the body, but then, within a few hours, you will recover a lot more energy from the outside.

External methods to help the Great Circulation

- One way to increase the sensation is to look at the path the energy takes and the main points from the spine through the arms and out through the hands. The path is linked to tendino-muscle meridians. The meridians end and start at these specific points, which are considered to be barriers. If you massage these points with acupressure or tap them with various Tui Na methods, the barriers will open and the passage will be freed.

- The best solution to free the path to the Five Gates circulation is taught in Daoist medicine.

- It is also possible to start training the Iron Shirt specifically for the Five Gate circulation. It is done more lightly than when you train it for martial arts. This is a way to stimulate the rise of the Yang (your Wei Qi) and also to reinforce the palm of your hand and free it from blocks.

All of these internal/external connections already exist and are natural. But we do not use them consciously, and this makes all the difference. Here we learn how to develop these qualities consciously in order to benefit from them. Thus, we transform something natural into something elaborate.

By training the stages above, you have started the Great Circulation, transforming Qi to nourish the mind. The more you exchange with the outside and purify your Yuan Qi (original energy), the more it develops your connection to Yuan Shen, the mind (something bigger than us), the spiritual part of your being. This connection is what triggers a lot of dreams and messages, and the impression of finally putting the pieces of a puzzle together, understanding major life concepts.

Being connected to both sides of the world
What is interesting about this stage is that you are still able to live a normal life without having to dedicate and sacrifice all your time to the practice. You can continue to work, have a family, watch TV... Nevertheless, at the same time, you start to have access to the spiritual, where you are connected and receive messages from something bigger. Your Hun (intuition, spirituality) is at its maximum potential and perfectly balanced with your Po (instinct, body, grounded in the world).

4. Transforming the mind to return to Dao (nothingness)

In this stage you continue to practice the Great Circulation and your regular training. At some point there is a transition made naturally and you enter the fourth stage by returning to the center, to oneness. The various facets of the mind stabilize into a unity. The Hun–Po/Yi–Zhi axis are balanced and the Shen is in the center of this equilibrium. As can be seen in the Human Map, each diagonal determines the qualities to develop in every aspect of the mind. Returning to the center is possible once the flaws have been worked on, problems are resolved, and the qualities are developed to their maximum potential.

> *There is one way to know you are at this stage: You experience at least one of the powers, abilities described in the Human Map. It may be receiving true messages in your dreams, or having an extremely refined understanding of the Way, or it may be that every aspect of life goes smoothly when something needs to be done, or the solution comes along at the same time, and so on. These manifestations are relevant and prove that you are no longer resisting change; on the contrary, you have become much more connected and in harmony with the Yi Jing (world changes) and true to the Way.*

At this point we have gone from a practice training and developing energy for greater vitality to a spiritual quest.

The Golden Path and Chong Mai

During the fourth stage, which generally lasts three years, the focus will be on bringing back to the center the qualities you have developed during the exchange with the world through the Small and Great Circulation. The center by then is well known since it will have been determined several times during the years of practice. The center is Chong Mai. By focusing the training on this central vessel, you will develop your Small Circulation and your exchange with the outside through a greater vertical axis going through you and continuing much higher and much lower than the body (Man between Earth and Sky). Therefore, the work on Chong Mai is a physical, emotional, and spiritual connection to what is greater, higher, and deeper than us.

This is what is called the Golden Path.

> *Note: Even though you are working on your alignment with a much higher vertical axis, you can still feel the front and back during the Small Circulation and the connection to the Five Gates remains, since the work on Chong Mai, going back to the center, gathers everything else. When you begin practicing, you start by training your alignment as it is the base of every technique. In the fourth stage, by focusing on Chong Mai—thus your vertical alignment with the universe—the circle is complete. It requires letting go of life as you have experienced it before, balanced between the practice and your daily life.*

You are now more in your practice (two-thirds) than in the mundane (one-third). You can no longer continue activities or have relations that are not consistent with your practice (a career you do not enjoy, people you do not care for); you will feel it and it will block you. You can only have this specific connection to Chong Mai if you have cleared your life of all the undesired elements. These are difficult choices that we often do not want to make.

The Golden Path connects you spiritually to the greater, and it is a mystical way that can be very satisfying. You can have esoteric experiences such as waking dreams and journeys. But here you are no longer dealing with the physical blocks that had to be worked on in the Foundations or the emotional blocks during the Transformation. Here you have to face the problems with the world and the choices that have to be made accordingly. You can only evolve on the Golden Path if your entire life goes in the same direction.

5. Staying in the Dao to crush the Dao (returning to the non-manifested chaos)

This is said to be a nine-year cycle, but in reality it is an end-of-life practice.

There is no choice left at this stage. The practice is life and life is the practice; the rest has disappeared. There is no real possibility of staying within the world as we know it. Even daily chores and necessities can no longer be performed. People (students, disciples) take care of you. You are no longer in the reality of the world; you have crossed to the other side.

In our tradition, we are not as interested in this stage because we prefer a life within the world and society. It is interesting, however, for us to catch a glimpse of the last process and come back to the world with more knowledge to teach and continue the training for perfect balance as a human being. Nevertheless, this *is* a possibility and the end of Nei Dan—a completed alchemic process. It is a spiritual quest, normally leading to death, with the concept of immortality and the conscious and luminous passage into the Yuan Shen (primordial spirit).

Immortality, in this sense, is the ability to be alive and at your best, or at least an evolution to fulfill your potential from the beginning to the end of life. It has nothing to do with the number of years you live. There is, however, a significant difference between your strength, mind, and appearance and your actual age. This is simply the manifestation of great vitality and good health thanks to all the Yang developed. Note that in traditional Chinese and Daoist medicine, if there are no blocks, there are no illnesses!

The importance of all the aspects—body, Qi, mind—in our system is very different from most other systems. If the three aspects are not balanced, nothing will work. If they are well balanced, each part helps the others. There is an accumulation of practices and synergy of them all: we need to practice more and to practice all of them.

Part Seven

Wai Gong
(Theory and Exercises for
Training the Body)

Chapter 13

How to Train the Qualities Developed through Physical Training

There are three main training categories corresponding to the Three Treasures: mind training or Shen Gong, body training with Wai Gong (external training), and Nei Dan (work on the breath). This trilogy represents the structure of Man between Heaven and Earth: Yang (Shen Gong), Yin (Wai Gong), and Yin–Yang (Nei Dan). We want to train these three aspects by breaking them down into five parts.

To go from Wai Gong to work Nei Dan, you need Nei Gong, which is a transition between pure body work and pure breath work. It is hard to sit still and work on the breath without pain or manifestation in the body if you haven't gone through the transition of Nei Gong. During body work your focus is set on the motion, and this is what you remember. In Nei Dan, however, the attention is solely on the breath. The idea in Nei Gong is to put your attention on your breath during a physical exercise. You no longer focus on the motion, which is now completely assimilated and natural, but on the sensation of breath during the motion.

- Wai Gong: attention on the body and movements.

- Nei Gong: same movements with attention on the breath and sensations.

- Nei Dan: you remain focused on the breath and sensation but you are now sitting down and still.

When you start training Shen Gong, although the focus is purely on the mind, you will have to deal with emotions that will invade your work. Xin Yi Dao Yin Fa is a specific training developed for this purpose—that is, stabilizing your emotions. Xin Yi Dao Yin Fa and Shen Gong, added to the Wai Gong, Nei Gong, and Nei Dan, compose the five facets of the training. These are linked to the Five Elements and also to Chinese astrology with the Ba Zi and Celestial Mandate. Indeed, the celestial stems and earthly branches perfectly coincide with each part of the training.

Body work is the aspect most often neglected, set aside in a spiritual practice, because body work is seen as basic work and not magic. But if the Yin is not trained, the Yang cannot go inside. The untrained body is a poor Yin that would be just like a pierced bucket that lets everything run out. The Yin has to be good quality in order to receive and hold the Yang inside.

It is just like a phone with a poor battery: it cannot store enough power.

Grounding, strengthening, and relaxing (coordinating) the body are the three main aspects of Wai Gong training. Strengthening and relaxing the body is pretty straightforward. Grounding the body, however, is more complicated as it requires two aspects: one is the instinctive, animalistic power and the other is the intuitive aspect much more linked to the soul. You cannot be grounded if you do not know who you are or if you doubt yourself. Indeed, grounding is a process that goes from physical to psychological training, from body to mind, and this requires a deeper level of training.

Training these four facets of Wai Gong—strength, co-ordination, physical grounding, and psychological grounding—will develop the physical structure.

Relaxation, coordination, and mobility

Being relaxed and coordinated is the capacity to be mobile and to have our body do what we want it to freely, without obstruction. It is also the capacity to reproduce any forms (within our physical limits) with no problem and limitation. The mind and the body are connected. In order to achieve this, there are many ways to train. There are many exercises to train coordination that are pointless in the long run and yet are necessary to acquire coordination. Once the muscle chains are trained in specific ways and dimensions, to move in a relaxed way, this stays with you all your life. Riding a bicycle may take a bit of practice, but once you know how to ride it, your body never forgets. And as soon as your body assimilates the exercise, you can forget it.

Mobility is slightly different in the sense that you can always push the body further and improve its capacities. Any kinesthetic exercise can be used for this. Once you are physically able to reproduce a motion, you then have to link the motion to a speed. This is the intent you link to the movement. The goal is to move your body in the most precise way and also at the fastest speed possible. Normally, since your mind is very fast, the body should be able to follow as quickly. Unfortunately, it is more complicated than that! The body's average speed is fixed by the time you are 12–13 years old. Nevertheless, even though the movement itself cannot really increase in speed, you can increase the speed in the very beginning of a motion.

Therefore, what will make a considerable difference is the motion's trigger point.

If you only train the starting point of a movement repeatedly, this corresponds to what we call Fa Jing. It is the explosive force that triggers the movement and gives the speed for the rest of the motion. Just like sneezing, you feel it coming and then it is sudden and explosive. The coordination and mobility only happen with a relaxed body. This implies having the mind and body linked, the mind being able to feel each part of the body and have it move in the way you want it to. If you are relaxed and coordinated, you can see a movement, analyze it, and reproduce it with no trouble.

Usually, seeing the movement is something everybody can do (unless you are visually impaired); understanding it is also something within most people's reach, although some people may need to see the same movement several times in order to understand it fully. These exercises do not require strength or great flexibility. But the difficulty comes in trying to reproduce what you see. This is mainly because we know how to analyze and take in the information, but when we try to recreate it, we are blocked by an accumulation of mental filters that paralyze the natural process of motion. Often the mind just reinvents a movement which is not quite the same. The mind needs to rationalize things. So if there is a movement you do not quite understand, your mind will automatically transform it to give the impression that it does understand it. Your image or memory of the movement in question is often very far from reality. This aspect needs a lot of training so the mind learns how to simply reproduce what it sees without the additional filters altering reality. This is the very meaning and purpose of Xin Yi Shuan: it is the thought form in motion. You think of a form and you do it immediately and exactly as thought.

These are very simple and clear motions which are usually performed in a linear way. With these exercises you will learn how to use the body as a whole in every movement. This aspect of physical training is linked to the intellectual part of the mind, the Yi. It is the capacity of following the movement. With this alone you can already get an interesting diagnosis on the state of your mind and body. You will immediately see what type of mental commentary appears while training—for instance, "This sucks. It is not at all what I want to do." This first comment simply states that you do not know how to actually do the movement in question. The ego is unhappy about its inability, so it prefers to criticize the exercise.

On the other hand, when you think what you are doing is great and then see yourself on video and realize how wrong you were, this is another way the ego works. The ego is so strong that it doesn't even try to get it right because it *knows* that it is right (in its own world)!

> *The harder it is to accelerate the movements and reproduce them quickly, the more power your mind has over you. The same thing occurs if your emotions are stronger and you are agitated. This means your ego and your mind control you.*

If you constantly repeat the same mistake over and over, this shows your mind's lack of clarity. Therefore, with a very simple exercise, you can already see very clearly what your problems are. But it also works the other way around! And this is where the Daoist vision of the balanced body, mind, and spirit proves to be extremely revealing and efficient when applied. If you see that your mind is not your tool and that it controls you, you will apply body exercises focusing on precision to train that aspect your mind. These exercises based on mobility will clarify your intellectual mind.

People who would really benefit from this type of mobility exercise actually run away from it because it is very irritating for the ego. Once you come to realize the problem, the good side is that you have these simple tools rather than trying to confront your mind directly to Shen Gong! Here it is just a question of repetition. For some it will be 200 times, for others 400; if it still doesn't work, just keep repeating the exercise and it will work eventually.

These coordination workouts are very useful in your daily life to clarify your mind before making important decisions, especially if you feel tense and irritated, and if you are questioning your actions. After one hour of these techniques, the mind will be much more available because it will be calmer and clarified. If it is not available because it is still rebelling against you, then add on an hour of training!

The point is: the body *can* hold the mind. This is the point of relaxation and coordination through mobility.

This is the advantage of long forms with internal martial arts. Once you are aligned and have a structure, you can also try to apply speed and explosion to the form. It is important to have both: to know how to move gently and precisely, and with great speed and power.

The Yi is your capacity to focus your attention. If you feel tired but still train, you will forget your fatigue as your focus of attention will have shifted on to the exercise. The stamina and speed, however, are linked to the other side of the horizontal axis called "Zhi" (linked to your Jing and fears). This is the second aspect in training your mobility. When training the Zhi, your exercise must last for a long time.

When you train the same exercise for a long period of time, you will be confronted with many issues. First comes boredom. This is a process that takes place even before any pain from repetition appears. Boredom is the way for the mind to refuse the exercise.

These exercises must be long but must also increase in speed. The idea is to go against what is natural for most of us—that is, starting out fast and strong, but gradually putting less power into the movement and also slowing down. These are the two most important components of Wai Gong: strength and mobility.

Isometric exercises are also a way to use the Zhi in order to increase body strength. This form of exercise reinforces the muscles and tendons; it also brings stamina to muscle mass. However, when you are not used to working this way, you do not want to overdo it because isometric exercises can strain the muscles and tendons if the work is not adapted to your capacity.

We need the Zhi to be strong and solid in order to maintain a good Yi (constant attention and fluidity in motion). And, the other way around, in order to train the Zhi, you must always keep a good sensation of your body, and this is possible with the Yi. So you work the Zhi and the Yi through the same training but from two opposite polarities: Yi (mobility) and Zhi (strength and stamina).

So, on the one hand, you have mobility and coordination, which will allow you to move in a relaxed way, and, on the other, strength, power, and stamina. This is what strengthens the body in Wai Gong. Then you have to keep the body aligned and grounded. These are the basic qualities that will develop a good structure. A good structure means good health. If you do not have a good structure, it is hard to work on the breath (Nei Dan) or on the mind in complete stillness (Shen Gong).

Once you know what it takes to build a good structure, you can identify these aspects in the range of exercises you are familiar with, and you can train these aspects consciously.

Everybody can train mobility. Just look at all the equipment available in gyms—cardio machines, weights, and so on. These machines work, but there is still something missing for a deep change. This is because the vertical aspect is missing. Indeed, we have looked into the horizontal axis with the Yi and Zhi polarities, but we also have to take into account the importance of the Hun and Po, which are the two polarities of the vertical axis.

Since Wai Gong is purely body work, if you do not add the intuitive and instinctive aspects to your development, the change will only be superficial. This is why we need the grounding, with exercises such as push and pull: pull with the Po and push with the Hun. When you pull using the Po, you bring back the strength to your center. It is a question of balance. The Po gives us the precise notion of where we are. And you cannot be grounded if you do not know where you are. You must be able to situate yourself in space very precisely in order to feel whether you are grounded or not. This is a quality developed through the Po.

And pushing with the Hun is a matter of being grounded. In order to be grounded, you need the tendons to be united. The tendons are part of the Hun. But the Hun and the Po work together, so you need both to be grounded. Strength and stamina are completely linked to Zhi. Mobility has to do with the quality of your Yi, but grounding is linked to the balance of your Hun and Po. The quality of physical grounding then becomes a psychological quality, but this is more difficult to obtain because it comprises many things.

Balance exercises are the most important to develop the qualities connected to the Po. Unfortunately, we have gradually lost our balancing skills because for too long we have based our balance only on vision. Vision is actually two-thirds of what we base our balance on! But vision is the sense that is the most linked to the mind and words—not to our ability to balance. In order to rediscover and develop the qualities of balancing based on feeling with a kinesthetic approach, you must cut yourself off from the visual space reference by closing your eyes during specific exercises. You can start by trying to keep your balance on one foot, the other foot slightly lifted in front or to the back. Slowly close your eyes and try to keep your balance with your eyes shut. This gradually connects your sense of balance to the kinesthetic rather than the visual. The only trouble with this exercise is that when you lift your foot, the center is not engaged. You are just resting on one leg, but you do not have the center for your gravity. In order to engage your center, you need to use your abdominal muscles and your spine. To do this, your knee has to be raised so that your thigh is horizontal to the ground. The third level of this exercise involves keeping in the same position with your hands behind your back; once your eyes are closed, move your head from right to left throughout the exercise.

In order for the Hun to develop and become grounded, you must train your balance through the kinesthetic approach. This implies that even if you are a talented surfer or tightrope walker and you have great balance, this will not be something that will develop your Hun, since the balance you have acquired is most likely based on your vision and not developed through kinesthetic work. Then, when you start training the actual grounding of the Hun, you will use two types of exercises: the static exercises (linking the tendons during a long period of time) and Fa Jings (explosive movements with tendons linking for a short period of time).

Static positions

If you use your strength, you can only stay in a static position for a limited amount of time. It is only when your tendons are connected and relaxed—grounded—that you can stay in the same position for hours. When you hold a static position, your body must stay slightly relaxed and this will naturally set your body the way it should be.

The basic and most simple level of static position is simply standing up straight and aligned with your arms relaxed alongside your body. If it is comfortable to do so, you can bring your arms forward as if they were embracing a big round belly. If this works well, you can raise your arms in the same rounded position up to chest level, as if you were embracing a tree trunk with your arms, and finally, if you are still comfortable, you can bring your arms above your head with the palms of your hands facing the sky.

These are the main static positions to develop your center. When you move from one arm position to another, you must stay aligned. This is what will develop Chong Mai, the axis that links Man to Heaven and Earth.

In order to find the perfect distance apart for your feet, the first thing you can try is going from one foot to the other, from right to left, lifting your foot up each time and letting it drop naturally. At some point your feet keep falling into the same position and this is the natural gap between your feet. Your feet have to be parallel and aligned with the width of your hips. If you do not feel balanced, you can move back and forth from the tip of your toes back to your heel; by rocking back and forth you will find a central point where you feel the most aligned.

The knees should be slightly bent, neither inwards nor outwards, but aligned with the center you found between your feet and in the direction of your toes. They are bent slightly forwards towards the feet and aligned with the hip. You must feel stable in this position. If you go down too far, you will feel your hips tip forward, which is something you do not want. Nor do you want to bend into a sitting position, pushing your buttocks back into a swayed position. You must feel your "guas," your hip area, aligned and lowered, pressing down into your knees and your feet, until you can no longer go further without jeopardizing your alignment.

> *Note: If your knees are straight rather than slightly bent, this means you will be aligned with your heels and not with the center of your feet.*

The same applies to the upper body: the armpits must be lowered in order to be aligned with the hips, and the arms must be aligned with the shoulders. Once you have found the center from hips to toes, you can relax and lower your shoulders into this alignment. The hands must be relaxed and below shoulder level. They shouldn't be in front or behind; otherwise, it would make your shoulders tense backwards or cave in forward. Once you apply all these steps to find your alignment, you simply stay still.

First static position

Once your feet are aligned, breathe naturally and after a while bring your hands forwards through your center and up, separating them into a rounded position, elbows out, as if you were holding the bottom of a big ball or holding a big belly.

Second static position

From this position, you push your elbows forward. This will naturally raise your arms. Stop when your hands are in the center of your chest. Make sure you feel the strength deriving from the pressure of your arms resisting outwards, forwards, above, and below.

Third static position

Once you have reached this point, you push your thumbs inwards, which will rotate your hands and wrists, and then push your little fingers towards the sky with your arms rising above your head, palms up (as if you were holding a ball in each palm).

Maintaining a static position has a settling, soothing quality. Once you have gone beyond the pain caused by tension at the beginning, it turns out to be a very pleasant and joyful practice. If you do not find pleasure in this and are always uncomfortable, it is probably because the position is incorrect. It is essential to keep things "open." This means making space in front of you, between your chin and neck, between your arms and body, and between your fingers. You should never tighten and close things up. Also keep in mind that your hands and fingers are connected: you must keep them in relation to one another.

Static positions can also be done sitting or lying down, although it is better to practice standing. The lying position will bring the circulation of Qi but will not bring enough change and movement to the body. And the goal here is to increase the flow of Qi.

Adding specific work to the static exercise

The first thing is to put pressure on the feet and push into the ground as if they were digging the earth. You try to find this sensation with the center and edge of your feet. You also add pressure to your knees by slightly pushing them forwards while separating them with a big imaginary ball. You need to make sure the muscles of your buttocks, abdomen, and throat are relaxed. When your buttock muscles are relaxed, gravity will naturally align your pelvis. Your attention should be on the physical aspect, focusing on each muscle from toe to head, making sure they are relaxed in this static position.

Obviously, since you are standing, you need your muscles to hold you, and therefore a slight tension remains. But you should be able to feel every one of them untighten and relax. You start from your feet, moving up to your ankles, shin muscles (tibialis anterior), calves, knees, thighs (especially the inside), stomach, buttocks, pectoral muscles, triceps, forearms, and hands. Maintain the structure while relaxing your muscles. Since it is hard to relax the neck, just make sure you focus your attention on it while moving up. Then focus and try to relax your jaw muscles, and finally place your attention on Bai Hui (top of the skull, on the central line, where it crosses the line connecting the top of your ears). You will probably have to go back and repeat this process because some muscles have a tendency to tighten almost automatically as a reflex. You will spend the entire time scanning your body over and over again from bottom to top.

Fa Jing

This is a repetition of short movements, which will accelerate until they reach an explosion—just like a sneeze. The whole body moves in one fast, powerful explosion. The hard thing about Fa Jing is to be able to condense the force in such a short time.

It is interesting to note that, in fact, the capacity of explosive force is developed through static training! But you can only train static positions if you are centered. And to be centered (balanced) you have to develop your Po.

You can see now how being grounded is something that has two polarities on a vertical axis: the Hun above (the most Yang aspect of the mind, intuitive, and related to the tendons) and the Po below (animalistic instinct).

The main qualities in Wai Gong are strength, relaxation, coordination, mobility, and grounding (with training of the tendons and balance).

With any given exercise, you should be able to train and develop these aspects above, essentially mobility and strength. Then you should try to train the same form with closed eyes or on an unbalanced support (for instance, training the form standing on a log). You can also train the form alternately tightening and relaxing the muscle chains that are involved in your motions.

With the qualities above in mind, you can examine the series of exercises you already train and look for the qualities that are most lacking in your practice. From there you can either change the way you train some of the familiar exercises or you can add other exercises to your practice. This mainly depends on your personal preference.

Nei Gong

Once you are comfortable with the purely physical requirements, you can start to focus on the sensation during training. For instance, you can notice the feeling of your skin in contact with the air, the difference between the inside of your body and the surface. You can also place your attention on your breath. This is when we shift from Wai Gong to Nei Gong. Nei Gong is the training of sensation and breath through any form in your practice.

There are obviously different qualities to Nei Gong than the ones we have just seen above in Wai Gong. The main two qualities of Nei Gong are:

1. the capacity to feel

2. the repeated capacity to feel.

Feeling

If you question your ability to feel, ask yourself if you are able to place your hand in front of you and, without moving it, feel each finger separately. Are you able to move your attention from one finger to the other and keep a clear sensation?

Our training aims to develop and educate this capacity.

Exercise 1: Develop your sensation

Here is a simple exercise to start developing your sensation.

In a sitting down position:

1. Move your hand forwards, pointing out at chest level.

2. Breathe in and bring your arm and palm towards you. Feel your hand.

3. Breathe out, extending your arm and hand out again, palm down, and increase the feeling in your hand.

4. Repeat this. Each time try to keep increasing the sensation in your hand.

It is interesting to note that even if you are able to perform this exercise, the feeling does not stay. It will dissipate fairly quickly. This is simply because you do not have enough energy to maintain the sensation. This is why, in order to increase the sensation and not lose it, you repeat the movement while breathing in and out. This also implies being able to focus long enough. After a while you can easily be distracted and are therefore not able to retain the sensation as clearly. The sensation can be on the entire hand or just on a small section, and can be any kind of sensation such as heat, cold, tingling, throbbing, pain, and so on.

Note: Just keep in mind that these sensations are not the energy itself but a manifestation of the difficulty of the energy circulating and trying to push through blocks—just like a cable will heat when electricity goes through. The heat is not electricity. The heat comes from the friction of the movement through the cable. The more painful it is or the more swelling you feel, the more your body is blocked with tensions. If the body has no blocks and energy flows through, you will have a very specific, indescribable sensation, very different from any of the manifestations above. The closest comparison would be something similar to an electrical current and a draft inside. If you are not able to feel your hand, you cannot train Nei Gong, and therefore you cannot train energy.

Exercise 2: Where do you feel the manifestation of energy?

The second step is to decide where you want to feel the sensation. This is why the sensation must be trained in order to feel it wherever you want. You can use the same exercise presented above. The difference is that here you aim to feel only *one* finger when you breathe out with your hand extended. This means you turn off the sensation from the other fingers and focus just on one finger. When you breathe in, you check the sensation on that finger—only that specific finger—and then, breathing out again, you switch fingers. You repeat this, "lighting up" one finger at a time. Sometimes you may choose to stay for a few breathing cycles on one finger, just to clarify your feeling, before bringing your hand back. You can also check the sensation when your hand is drawn back during several breathing cycles, but once again you breathe out when you extend your hand, while changing from one finger to another. Make sure you do not move the chosen finger more than the others. The fingers should not be in motion. If this works for you, this means you can move on to the next step.

Exercice 3: Going from one hand to the other
Breathe in with the sensation on your hand; breathe out with the sensation on one finger; breathe in, bringing your hand back with the sensation on your finger; and breathe out, switching hands and focusing your attention on the same finger on the other hand (the one you have just extended). Bring it back and breathe out with the same hand but a different finger. Breathe in and change hands, focusing on the same finger on this extended hand. For instance, if you were focusing on your right-hand index finger, when you switch to your left hand, focus on your left index finger.

> *This is very simple kinesthetic training, but it is essential to develop this capacity for the practice of Nei Gong.*

The third aspect of "feeling" is the notion of *depth* in front of your hand.

There is a difference in sensation depending on whether you place your hand in front of you or towards the ground, in front of a wall, in front of a person, on top of a table, or on top of your thigh. This differentiation also has to be trained. At first it is easier to train with obvious elements. For instance, you can compare the feeling between your hand on your thigh and your hand in the air. You will immediately feel the warmth emanating from your body as opposed to the cold from the air. This ability will be useful when you practice Chinese medicine and martial arts, but unfortunately it is not developed through our general practice. You have to train it specifically. This is the only way to educate your hand's sensation.

Later, when you will be asked to have a sensation penetrate deep inside, the notion will remain vague if you have not trained the basics first. You can't just imagine what's inside to get there! You need to know how to feel depth. The first exercises are all about finding the difference in sensation with your hand: your hand surrounded by emptiness, your hand far from a chosen object, your hand close to an object, and so on. This could be compared to using your hand like a sonar.

Nourishing the sensation

When you focus on the feeling in your hand, it is not passive. You actually nourish the sensation by pulling up, breathing through your center, and then breathing out towards your hand.

This is reversed breathing, in which you pull in your abdomen and pull up the perineal muscles while inhaling. Once you have chosen your focus of attention, you let go of your abdomen and perineal muscles, and you concentrate on the chosen spot. Your intention will bring the sensation to that point. If you do it right, it should enhance the sensation with tingling from your core to your hand.

> *Note: The energy needs an arrival point. It does move, but you cannot push the energy from one point to another. You must think of your core and the chosen spot—in this case, your finger.*

The Zhi is the element solicited in the repetition of this exercise, using your center to enhance the sensation in your fingers. You should be able to repeat the cycle at least 100 times. And this implies increasing your sensation at each cycle rather than having it gradually fade away. This is determined by the amount of energy you have and your capacity for endurance based on the Zhi. This is a bit harder because it requires more energy than in the first exercises. Consequently, if you do not have enough energy, it won't work.

Nevertheless, you are not depleting your energy. In fact, you use your energy only to have it come back to you stronger.

We have seen the two major qualities that should be trained:

- The sensation that develops the Yi.

- The movement of energy with a specific point of focus which develops the Zhi.

Expanding and condensing

The two other major qualities in Nei Gong are "expanding" and "condensing" the energy.

The expansion of energy is easy to feel: the more you train sensation, the more you will feel that your energy is expanding and gradually moving further and further out of your body and around. This happens naturally. The only problem with this is that you become a heater for your surroundings, but you do not heat your own center as the energy does not go towards you—on the contrary, it moves out. You need this Yang energy to come back inside to nourish you. This is when you need to be able to "condense" the energy. This is not a natural process. You must develop a very specific sensation. In order to do this, you must first identify your bone mass.

Condensing exercise

First, start with your hand. Breathe in while focusing on feeling your bones. Breathe out by condensing, pressing the feeling into your bones. Breathe in again and identify your hand's bone mass; breathe out and bring the feeling you have in your hand into your bones. You will quickly have the impression of having a heavy hand.

When you condense, you bring the sensation towards the center into the bone marrow. You need to have a good sensation of your skeleton for this. It is best to start with your hands and arms. Once you truly find the sensation of condensing into the hand bone, it will then develop naturally in other parts of your body. You can even start with a finger and focus on bringing the entire sensation of the hand into the finger bone. This can be done moving, still, or sitting down. On the one hand, you have the sensation from your breath that expands the energy and the sensation outwards, and, on the other hand, you bring the energy back in by condensing it into the center.

You need both for the practice to be complete. Condensing corresponds to the Po, which is linked to the metal element. Expanding corresponds to the Hun, which is linked to the wood element.

Part Eight

Some Final Words

Conclusion

It is important when you start training to understand what you are really working on. You may be more focused on training the martial arts or on the health aspect. At some point you have to know what we do. We are in a lineage with a very clear tradition. This tradition is a personal training tradition. It is a spiritual training in the sense of development—not religious but as in a tradition that trains what is really inside us. For this you have to know how my school works. It is very important as we have a very old and practical system. It is about developing the human being as much as possible. It has nothing to do with China; it can apply to any country and culture, because the focus is on developing our qualities as human beings.

Before, you might have trained for a long time and eventually the teacher would tell you the actual structure of the style—why we train certain aspects this or that way, why it has been designed in this way, and what the different parts are and how they go together.

But today, especially with the Western mind, it is good to have both. You have a training where you come to follow your calling and you follow what the instructor says, and you just absorb the information by doing it. But it is actually good at the same time to have the meaning behind the exercises and explanation of why we train in specific ways.

If we understand how it was designed in the beginning, then we understand the logic of it and we then we see what we need, which aspect is necessary for our development. Usually, a good tradition is complete, whole by itself. You shouldn't have to go elsewhere to find information to perfect it.

Within the name of our tradition, the Ba Men Ziran Fa system, or Da Xuan, which means the Big Secret, there are eight doors to reach the "natural state." In Chinese, this expression of "natural state" is not the idea of being natural and spontaneous as we might explain it in English, but what is perfect inside (Zi) enabled to come out (Ran). You free what is perfect inside.

Many spiritual practices talk about this concept (the Buddha Natural, for instance). Here we do not practice to add on to our condition; on the contrary, we practice to get rid of things that bother us. In the *Dao De Jing*, Chapter 40, it is explained that the movement of Dao is going back to simplicity. Even the Bible talks about the "simplicity of a child." This does not mean you should do foolish things like a child. It means that after all your practice and the accumulation of all your knowledge you want to go back to acting in a simple way. You understand things and you do them. You do not have to go through the process of questioning and commenting on your actions.

There is a major difference between Daoism associated with Buddhism and Daoism which is a clan–family system where the practitioners remain few in number and only transmit to the people they know. They consider the San Bao—the Three Treasures—as the ancient tradition did—that is, the body, the mind, and vitality (Jing, Shen, and Qi) or, more concretely, the body, mental mind (intellectual), and breathing exercises (which is the same as vitality and Qi).

The Jing, the essence, carries a lot of concepts, but it is mainly the body. The body is the container in which you will put all the good stuff. If the container is weak, you cannot use it. Furthermore, the training consists in a lot of things. If the training lasts a long time, then this implies that you have to stay healthy a long time, thus having a strong body. Otherwise, you cannot train. You cannot meditate if you have the flu or a headache.

As a spiritual and personal practice, every system has one problem at the beginning, which is motivation. Why do you start this type of training? To get stronger because I like martial arts, because I want to get healthier, reduce stress, and so on.

We have to understand something. If you were to go to the old-style master today and ask him, "Why should I train? Why should I spend my precious time training?" the answer would simply be "Don't!" Because what we want to do in the practice is actually eliminate the need for this question of "Why should I train?" This question is actually the problem. It is the need for motivation that keeps bringing up this question. But the thing you learn with a long-term practice is that any motivation, even with the best intentions, is always wrong. Good motivation for practice does not in fact exist.

> *Practice should be practice because it is practice. It is the free aspect of practice that is the way you explore the real meaning of life.*

Of course, we all have our motivations at the beginning, but this is never good and at some point you practice just because you practice, in the same way that this is the reason you brush your teeth or you wash daily. It is just the way to make yourself feel better and to mix more easily with people. A personal practice is a path—Dao means a path, a road—and you can live your life very well without a path. It is like a map when you arrive in a new city. A map will come in handy. Then again, it all depends on the type of map. You have two kinds of bad map.

The first map is over-complicated, like an army map overloaded with information and details. This makes it so confusing for the person who is new to the city that it will not help. Then you have the tourist map which only includes the major sites and a few main streets. This does not help because too much information is missing.

Our tradition is the same. Too much information and too many details make it difficult to practice, because you are always correcting yourself and wondering what you are doing wrong. If, on the other hand, you are told to just sit and wait because "it will come," this will definitely not work either! You actually need to do stuff! Or someone might say, "Do the form and you will know how to fight." No! It does not work that way. You have to fight to fight. In the practice, not only do you have a map but you also need a guide. You do not want a teacher who can talk about it for hours but does not practice. When you are hiking up a mountain, it is better to have someone from the mountains who lives in these conditions rather than someone who did research and wrote a book about mountains. It is good to be educated and knowledgeable about your practice, but you have to actually have trained and done it all as well. Whichever aspect you train in the system, you always have to make sure the person who guides you has trained the same aspect so that you can ask him thoroughly about the details and questions that arise when you practice. The older the tradition is, the more answers they have for all aspects of the practice. Sometimes you do not want to hear the answer! But the answer will be there! The guide should always be able to give you the right path.

Traditionally, we use the example of a temple. When you start practicing, it is like building a temple. First you have to find the space and where you want to build it. In your life this is finding the ideal timing, when you are not distracted by things, when you are stable enough, and when you have the right people around you.

Then you go in and you have to clean up a little to make space, just as you have to make space and time in your daily life to train. Then you need to make the space special. So it is in your practice, which becomes ritualistic at the beginning in that you separate it from the rest of your day by making a special time for it. This is motivating at first, but then you realize that if you do this, the practice and your life are so far apart that they never mix. Very soon you start to practice between other elements in your daily life—before taking your shower in the morning, when you come back from work, before you make dinner, before you go to bed. By making the practice part of your life, it will actually start to change your life and help you evolve. The breathing and the way you stand and move in the practice start to seep into your life, and soon there is no more separation. Just like the temple that becomes a place where you pray but also the place you live in, a place where it is natural to be. You want to defend this palace, which is natural and complete, by making it strong, by staying healthy, but also defending the space from intruders. You made the temple really nice and you don't want stupid people to come and break everything. So it is important to defend it too. In my tradition we say that you cannot have a normal relationship with people if you are scared. Half of the practice is on your own, but the other part is interacting with people. If you are scared, tense, and anxious, it is very difficult to interact naturally. This is why you need to make sure you can defend yourself and be able to defend your opinions, staying relaxed since you are no longer scared of people's reactions.

The body is as important as the mind and vitality, so we need to be relaxed in order not to be scared. Then you can start to share and invite people in. People will see the change in you and will be attracted by what you are doing. By your example you attract people to the practice. When you behave well and are better with other people, you create a nicer world—the environment around you. Then you are able to go elsewhere to meet people who have done the same and share with them.

From the year 200, as well as Daoism in China there was also Buddhism. The two mixed together for a long time, The Daoists started going in monasteries only because Chinese people would go to the shaman for life rituals—burials, for instance. The rituals were very simple, and the people began to see the Buddhist tradition come in with fancy clothes and music for the rituals, and they were simply more attracted to what seemed nicer and more ritualistic to them. The Buddhists gained popularity very quickly and the Daoists started to copy the Buddhists. At one point after the Tang Dynasty it was the same thing. But the clan or family Daoist tradition could not mix because the training in their tradition was very different from the Buddhist training. So a small family tradition maintained their own way, and this is what we practice today.

These are the five aspects of the practice that we need to train in order to have a complete practice:

- External training, which is the pure physical body training—Wai Gong.

- Internal training, which involves the same movements done long enough so that your intent switches from analyzing the motion to the sensation of structure with breathing—Nei Gong.

- Pure breathing in a completely still seated position— internal alchemy, Nei Dan.

- Xin Yi Dao Yin Fa, which is a kind of relationship between the body and the thinking that becomes emotion.

- Pure mind training—Shen Gong. The mind becomes your tool and you are no longer the tool of your mind.

Destiny

Today we could translate this term as "applied psychology." The idea is that if I better understand the people I talk to, I am better able to make them understand my concept. If I understand the main characteristics of different types of people with astrology— Ba Zi (the eight characters, and understanding each aspect of the person through the Five Elements and Yin/Yang aspects) and Zi

Wei Du Shu (also astrology)—I can then understand how to talk to those people. My interaction with them will be easier if I know how to talk to them. We have a precise understanding—a map of the mind (developed later). You can see in its different aspects how to approach and reach out to more people when they are anxious, make them feel safe, and so on.

Destiny is understanding ourselves and other people, knowing how we can connect.

Divination

For a long time in Daoism, laws were used to understand things that happen. The Five Elements, Yin–Yang theory, the Ba Gua, and Yi Jing (the Book of Changes, of simplicity) are the theories used for this. Change is actually what is the most simple (the natural way things are supposed to be). With the Yi Jing, you understand the changing of the world of the seasons, of your own emotions, of the battlefield. All the Yin–Yang lines, stacked together to give the 64 hexagrams (Gua), will actually have six possibilities of change on each of the lines, which give you an explanation of pretty much everything.

Divination is Yi Jing. All the laws of interaction in Daoist medicine, astrology, Ba Zi, and Zi Wei Du Shu come from the Yi Jing.

Medicine

Medicine is very important because you cannot train if you are not healthy. Also, because our training lasts for a long time, we need to stay healthy. Our tradition is situated in life, in contact with other people; if other people are not feeling well, we think about it and we do not feel good ourselves, so it is important to know how to make them feel better. You need to know how to fix little problems, for yourself and others. Chinese medicine is very structured and precise, and if you understand its concepts, even if you are not very good, you can use the needles and achieve results.

Daoist medicine is more holistic and magical. We go to the center of the problem, but the efficiency depends on the person doing it! This means that the skill of the practitioner determines the quality of the treatment.

Observation

When you look at yourself and train yourself, you start to look at other people. When you look at others, you realize all the different levels of interaction with different people. You realize we all live in our surroundings, and you start to look at your surroundings through Feng Shui and geomancy, and try to see, if we understand ourselves and the others, how can we make our surroundings as good as they can be for us and the others.

Once again based on the Five Elements and the Ba Gua, when you see that such a person has this type of energy, then you make the space around you as perfect as possible. In our tradition one specific aspect of this is morphopsychology.

This is quite complicated. What you need to do first is work on the five aspects that will make you better. It is only when you can better understand yourself and all the aspects of yourself that you can start to look at other people and your surroundings. First you must concentrate on yourself, for yourself.

Practice is always when you are alone. When you are in the school as a group, you train together to correct and learn, but this is never your actual training. Practice is only by yourself for yourself. In our path there are two aspects that should be balanced. You have to correct yourself; you must always keep learning and evolving. And, on the other hand, there is the practice. You let go of the corrections and you just practice. If you don't let go of the corrections, even with a good heart and good intentions, you will not be truly practicing, and you can stay the same for years with no true evolution. If you do not practice, you do not evolve.

This is a very simple Yin–Yang concept. It can explain everything and the way we train. If you train and stop, you realize you have a lot of energy but the energy goes away, because when you train you have a tendency to create Yang energy, and Yang energy goes up. You will feel warm and you can even warm up the room. But you want to keep this energy and not just be a heater for the room! If you go back to the Yin–Yang theory, it gives you an answer on how to train. Yang is more an action than Yin, but Yang is also subtler than Yin. It can be the mind. If I build a table, preparing myself to build it is Yin and building the table is Yang. But we could also say that thinking and planning the construction is Yang, and materializing the plan by building it is Yin. So how do you train for the Yang energy to stay in your body? Action is Yang, and the body, the structure, is Yin. You want to transform your body structure with Yang because you cannot transform with Yin. You need the Yang action to transform the Yin structure. You cannot just stand immobile, stare at yourself in the mirror, and develop your body. If you take a weight and start lifting it with your arms, using your biceps muscle, the Yang action will make the Yin, the structure, move. If you do it for a little while, your arm will be warmer. But it doesn't change the structure. But if you continue your exercise long enough and with the correct intensity, the Yang motion will change the Yin structure. You gain muscle as the Yin, transformed by the Yang, becomes better Yin. This better Yin can do more Yang motions, which will keep improving the Yin until it reaches the best it can be, which is your Jing (the hidden root). Then at some point your Yang and your Yin are at their best and you are at the maximum of your ability.

Then you can move on to the next point.

Every aspect has key words to remember what we are really looking for. The most important thing when you start training is to know what you are looking for. When you train your body, you need to look at three things:

1. Strengthening

One thing that will come by itself when you train every day is *strength*. Not in the way that a bodybuilder gains strength, but by becoming stronger because you are using your body much more as a whole. Everything you do then seems easier because you are more aligned and coordinated, and using your body more wisely.

> *Note: When you are stressed, you put much more tension in your body and use much more strength than you need in little daily motions. You can imagine the energy wasted for this. An experiment measured the force used by the most stressed university student while eating soup. He was using the equivalent of 7 kilos of force to bring his spoon of soup up to his mouth!*

If you use your body as a whole for all your daily actions, you will not be wasting energy, and this is why you feel more vitality and strength. You are not yet gaining energy. This will happen after some time when your continuous Yang training changes your Yin structure. Then you are *actually* getting stronger.

This increased strength is abundance of Qi. This "excess" of vitality is very beneficial because each time you get sick the symptoms mean your body is defending itself. When they start training, a lot of people complain, "I was never sick before. How can I get sick now that I am doing something good for my body?" In fact, before, your defensive energy was not strong enough to fight so the illness would gradually seep in deeper and deeper. When your Qi is empty, you don't fight, but the illness just makes you function at a lower level and then gradually keeps on bringing you further and further down. You don't feel it, but it becomes deeper and worse. In contrast, just like children, the slightest cold will bring high fever and so on. Each time you get sick, all the symptoms are signs that your body is defending yourself. You no longer have this gradual deficiency when you train; each time there is a problem, your body fights to get back to zero.

Also, being strong means that this abundance of Qi will solve other daily problems: you will not feel tired, you will sleep better, you will digest much faster, and so on. According to the Chinese Daoist concept, it is not the muscles that give strength; rather, they are the vector for tendons. The actual use of force is with the tendons. This is why in our tradition we concentrate on training the tendons and use a lot of twisting and turning in our motions. This is what gives the specific strength.

2. Relaxing

Becoming loose and relaxed means that the body functions as a whole and you have no tension in motion. This implies coordination. If you see someone doing a movement that does not challenge your normal ability (as opposed to a gymnast doing backflips!), then you should be able to watch and reproduce the movement. It should not be difficult for your body to reproduce something you understand and that is within your reach physically. But if you realize that after one hour of trying you cannot do it, this means that there is a problem of proprioception and coordination. These two qualities are directly linked to the fact of being really relaxed or not. Normally, if your mind understands and your body works, the two together should be able to reproduce the motion.

There are many of these plans of motion that are not connected properly between mind and body. This is the first hurdle, when people realize their lack of coordination. This is when the first people leave! Being relaxed is what keeps you healthy. When you are clear as to what comes from your mind, what comes from your body, and the connection between the two, everything goes more smoothly.

3. Grounding

Being physically grounded means that if someone pushes you or pulls you, you stay there. This is something we train a lot. In fact, this training does not remain something purely physical. If I am really grounded, I realize that emotionally, and even with my mind, I am more grounded. This is very important because when we train we go through a lot of emotional challenge; it helps if you have a lot of grounding. As soon as you start energetic work you can quickly lose track of reality and become a bit disconnected. The grounding is crucial for this because it creates the necessary balance for the spiritual work. Otherwise, it can really go wrong! It is not good to be too mundane, but it is even worse to be too disconnected.

In our system, we need to defend and occupy our space. We have to be there. And to be there we must be grounded. This is also very important for martial arts.

Grounding, relaxing, and strengthening are the three aspects we train in the body work.

Each part of our practice—breathing, Shen Gong, Nei Gong—has several aspects that have to be trained, and these are also defined by key words. Again, these are given so that we can understand what we are looking for.

We can make it pretty simple. When you train for yourself, you want to develop a couple of things as soon as you start the practice.

1. Feeling

I need to learn how to *feel*: not only feel my body in space, but feel the warmth of my hand in the cold air, feel the difference between my muscles, tendons, and bones. It goes from very simple things such as feeling your body in motion, in space, to more subtle aspects such as the feeling around your hand depending on where it is. There is a difference, for instance, between the sensation when your hand is a few inches from your thigh and a few inches from the ground. If you train long enough, the feeling becomes more acute and you can feel major differences. When you train, you can feel the difference between training alone and having people next to you.

This is also very useful in medicine and martial arts. We need to feel as much as we can during the day and as soon as we train. When you feel tingling or warmth, cold pain, or swelling in your body, this is *not* energy. It is the energy trying to flow into something that is completely blocked. The true feeling of energy it is something very smooth and not manifested. This can be compared to electric current in a cable: it is not the electricity that creates the heat but the friction of the current trying to go into something that is trying to resist it.

2. Linking

My body needs to be linked as one. This means that if I move my arm, the movement is in fact coming from my back, my hips, my legs, my feet on the ground. Even if I sit down and push my arm up, the motion has to come from the rest of my body and from the ground. Any motion has to be linked. My body should not move as if each part was cut off from the others. The whole body has to participate in every movement as one. This is how we save energy.

In order to train this, we start with very easy things such as squeezing the fist and seeing which tendons and muscles we tighten like a chain in the rest of our body. Later, the body is able to feel without the need for clenching, with just a little tension in the hand tendons to help sense the connection. We call this exercise "grabbing," which is exactly what you do at the beginning.

3. Grounding

We need to be grounded for energy. If your Yin structure is weak and not grounded, the Yang energy generated from the exercises will just go away. In order to keep the energy, you have to store the energy. That is the concept of inner alchemy. It has to stay inside. And for this we need grounding. Every motion has a direction and a relationship to the earth you are standing on. One of the main exercises to train this quality is the "push and pull" with a fellow student. Here, you understand how to use the ground with your front and back leg, without moving your feet, in order to push and pull your partner and resist his attempts to push and pull you. This means that if you want to go forward (push), you need to feel your back leg, and if you want to go backwards (pull), you need to feel your front leg. If you apply this concept, you can train the grounding quality in any movement. You must have the feeling and contact with your legs when you are training in any position. The intention is 70 percent leg and 30 percent hand in training!

We can also call the push and pull "absorb and project." When you push and absorb, you can train with one foot in front of the other. You absorb by pulling your arms towards you and going back with your front leg, then you sink in and project by pushing your arms forward, using your back leg. When you are pushing with your back leg or pulling with your front leg, you always need to stay aware of the moment when you are actually no longer using your leg. This is considered falling, and you always need to make sure you do not reach that moment. When you do this exercise, you can add another quality, which is feeling. As soon as you start, you want to feel the warmth of your hand against the cool air and the difference between the front and back of your hand. Later you can develop this feeling to your arm and your entire body, but it is good to start with your hand. When you pull, it is not at all the same feeling in your hand as when you push. Then you add breathing. When you inhale, you pull; when you start to exhale, you push. You follow your natural breathing pattern without trying to extend your breath according to the movement. You will notice that it is not at all the same feeling when you inhale as when you exhale.

Now we can add a third quality: grabbing. When you pull, you squeeze your arm, forearm, shoulder, chest, and dorsal muscles; when you push, you open your hand and add tension with the tendons so that you can feel the pressure in the movement, and repeat this. You have your grounding exercise during which you feel and link your body. Here are the three qualities in one motion.

You can test these qualities in martial arts, but it can quickly become aggressive. The grounding exercises are fun and you really change the most important aspect of the training, which is grounding. It is good for health and for basic spiritual development. You need your body to be strong and firmly on earth, because the more the Yang energy rises, the more the body needs to be grounded.

Keep in mind the major concept of Daoism of Man between Sky and Earth! Energy of Heaven is Yang and energy of Earth is Yin. Everything that is Yang will have a tendency to rise; everything Yin will have a tendency to go down. Between there has to be a good balance of Yin and Yang. If one is higher, then that is what you call sickness.

These are the three qualities we need to train for external and internal training.

It is also important to understand the Yin and Yang concept to establish not only which training is good for us but also what types of food and so on.

When you start training, first you need the basics. With your teacher or instructor, you receive information and you just have to follow. Then, by doing, the teaching comes into you a little and this gives you enthusiasm. If you do not find enthusiasm and still have to force yourself to train after years of practice, then there is a problem. Indeed, the teaching, Yang, comes into you by the practice, Yin, so the teaching that you make your own brings Yang out—Fire, and thus Joy and happiness. And then the problem is to find the right balance between Yin and Yang. If you do too much, you burn out; if you do too little, nothing works.

We compare training to cooking: it is the "fire regime." There is only one thing we know for sure with the training. It is like boiling water. If you have just a bit of heat under the pan or high heat, it can take more or less time to boil—but it will eventually boil. However, if you keep taking the pan of water off of the burner before it boils, it will never boil. This means that even if you train a little, that's OK, but you need to train every day. There is no weekend or Sunday off when it comes to training! Training is a way to be. The only thing we know is that we have to train all the time, and then the water boils. The problem is knowing how much fire we need. You go from getting the information, training the information, getting the knowledge to be yourself, finding enthusiasm and using it to really train and then regulate the training. After a while, training too much can be as bad as not training enough, because at some point you just burn out. Some people need to burn out to find their balance, but it is better not to go too far because it takes a very long time to recover. You can even get tendon problems and inflammations because your structure (Yin) cannot stand the motion (Yang), especially when you are undertaking martial arts training with weapons. Too much Yang will cause inflammation. On the other hand, if you do not do enough, your body will become flabby with an accumulation of Yin—fat. If you are too Yin, you can no longer ignite the Yang.

> *Note: This is why it is very important to understand the Yin–Yang concept. And indeed we have a manual to explain this: the Yi Jing. The Yin Jing, as we know it in existing books, is not the Yi Jing as the comments of the hexagrams and their lines are based on Confucian theories, which are far from Daoism. This third-level understanding can be interesting culturally, but this does not help us in our practice. This is why I tried to make an old-style Yi Jing in English; in fact, this is an internal alchemy manual with the concept of Yin and Yang.*

Nei Dan

In Nei Gong exercises you concentrate on your feeling and breathing. Internal training, Nei Dan—internal alchemy—

transforms your vitality through breathing. Nei Dan is practiced sitting down—there is *no* motion.

The major part of Nei Dan is feeling your breathing in your body. For this we have to train. We always start with the lower abdomen (lower Dan Tien, two fingers beneath the navel). When you breathe in, you feel that area, and when you breathe out, you feel the same area more precisely, warmer, more swollen. Then you repeat this cycle, making the feeling more and more precise. The belly is soft, without too much muscle, so this is a place where the Qi is less felt. In fact, it is the most difficult. In order to train the sensation, it is better to start with places that are less fatty and with a lot of bones and tendons—ideally your hands.

With the hand it is much easier. When you know how to do the basic Nei Dan exercises with your hands, you can then do the same exercises with your center. At first, sitting down, you just want to feel the difference of sensation in your hand when you breathe in and when you breathe out. You just focus on one hand and forget about the other one. When you inhale, you try to feel one finger, without moving it. When you exhale, you want to increase the feeling of your finger. Inhale again and see what you just did and go back to the feeling. Exhale and accentuate the feeling in your finger. The finger you choose should be the one really warming. You don't want the whole hand and the whole thigh to feel the same way. If you want to feel your finger more easily, it will help if your body is relaxed (one of the qualities seen above) and also linked. In order to do this, you can put a bit of tension in your finger so that the tendons are linked with the rest of your body.

Keep in mind how important it is to be relaxed because any action you perform is a use of Yang energy. If you are relaxed when you do the exercise, you will consume much less than if you are in a tense position. Think of the pictures of Buddha meditating with a faint relaxed smile.

Note: In fact, a study in 2007 proved that when you pretend to smile, almost as much good information reaches your brain as when you really are smiling. So the good chemicals in the brain are there also when you pretend to smile!

On the other hand, when you have a straight, contracted, angry face, it is using your energy and can actually make you sick! The face and the attitude have to be open, which will lead to relaxation. The most important thing you have to look for when you breathe is not technique, but just the simple pleasure of breathing.

The first thing a good breathing practice brings you is vitality. Breathing, vitality, and energy are all the same. The breathing aspect is what is closest to the human aspect in the concept of Man between Heaven and Earth. The mind (Shen) is Yang; the Jing, the structure, is Yin; and the breathing is Yin–Yang. What is Yin–Yang and causes us trouble? Our emotions. This is the closest element to Qi. This means that the breathing technique is the closest you well get to solving your emotions.

Note: When you are overwhelmed by an emotion, it is already too late; there is nothing you can do and it will not help to start your breathing then!

The only thing you can do is train yourself not to have this emotion take over again. But you are the way you are and you cannot fight emotions. This is how the training can help so that the emotion does not come back in the same way. The breathing exercise is the first level of all emotional training. If you have an extremely good breathing technique, you can digest your emotions better. Emotions are never negative if they can come to an end: "I am really sad but then it is done." But the way we are and the way our mind works today makes the emotions linger on. The main reason is that we are not in survival mode any more, so when an emotion arises it has time to develop and time to be commented on, which then leads to another emotion. This is endless. This is what creates moods. Long-term emotion is considered to be the first cause of internal disease in traditional Chinese medicine.

The breathing technique is supposed to do what you want. This is why is important to train the sensation in specific parts, such as one finger, to direct your intention clearly. All the other internal alchemy techniques are very interesting, but they require so many things that are difficult in everyday life. But for your own health and vitality and to gain energy, you do not need the actual Nei Dan. The basic breathing technique is sufficient for this—that is, finding the center and having a close relationship with your breathing. First you look for the feeling in your finger and then you do the same thing with the center by putting one palm on your navel and the second palm over the first one. The Lao Gong point at the center of the palm covers Qi Hai (the point about two fingers down from your navel) and Lao Gong on the second palm covers the first. Relax the shoulders, inhale, feel your center, and exhale, going into the warmth and making it stronger and more intense; inhale and notice the sensation, with your intent placed exactly on the point you want, and exhale, increasing the sensation and making sure your intent is on the right spot. If you do not feel anything, just focus on your hands. Since Nei Dan is a retreat to your center, a Yin practice, having your eyes closed is better. If, however, you fall asleep when you close your eyes, then you can look at a plain wall, or you can sit on the edge of a chair. Once you find the feeling with this exercise, you do exactly the same, keeping your intent on the center, but this time letting your hands rest on your thighs. At first, using products such as essential oils or tiger balm can help by increasing the sensation on the center when you no longer have your hands placed on your Dan Tien.

Many books on Nei Dan are very detailed on the use of certain points and are very technical. These techniques work very well for transforming the Yang, but when you begin, due to their technical aspect, you never really let go because you are concentrating on doing it the correct way. Therefore, you are never really completely letting go in the practice and for this reason it will not work.

You actually do not need anything other than the breathing technique. The only thing that it does not cover is the use of vitality to help the emotional side. This is why we need Xin Yi Dao Yin Fa for emotions. As for the amount of time you train, even five minutes a day is better than nothing and will help you not fall out of practice. However, it will not help you evolve. If you want to actually improve, there are minimum lengths of time. The Wei Qi (outside Qi) will go all around your body in 30 minutes (in fact, a little more than 28 minutes), which means that if you practice for 30 minutes, the whole body will be nourished by the training. But if you do breathing for 30 minutes, part of the time is wasted by getting into the exercise, so in fact you need more. You need 30 *real* minutes to increase your stamina. The same is true if you want to change your body and mind. Then the complete training should be minimum of one and a half hours a day—30 minutes each for body, Qi, and mind. After a while, when you know how to make all these aspects unite into one, it requires less time.

The most important thing in Nei Dan is finding the pleasure in breathing. The rest will come later. Do not be tricked by the heating and the center. The first thing is to breathe and to stay in one spot in your body. If you are in pain or injured in any way, the breathing will help. When you inhale, you pick the painful spot; as you exhale, you dive into it. The pain will expand and become quite intense, but then it will fade much faster. You are really healing yourself. This also works for emotions and trauma. If you are feeling very sad, for instance, dive into the feeling with the same technique and it will go away much faster. Before dissolving the problem, however, this technique will nourish it! Whatever the problem is, it will become more intense during the exercise.

But then when it is done, it is done. This capacity of putting your intent in a specific spot in your body and also moving it is very interesting for all the aspects above.

> *Note: This is not meditation, even though many people think it is. Meditation only concerns the mind, the immaterial, and thoughts. As soon as you are in your body and feeling it, this is no longer meditation but Nei Dan. Because the term "meditation" had been overused and carries so many connotations, I prefer not to use it. Thinking is not real—thinking is in your mind. When you think, physiologically it does not change a thing. If it goes into your system, it is because it created friction from unfinished thoughts that linger on. This creates emotions.*

Emotion comes from the Latin "emovere," meaning moving from the center. This implies that the emotions go from the mind into the body. Chains of thought create a little chaos. Then the energy will change and this change will create a change in your body. Your body will send a message to your mind to let it know something has changed and then you will recognize it as a specific feeling. But the emotions are already there. They are manifested in the body. If our thinking is clear, we have a lot of thoughts and only some become emotions. Once again, because of the way we have evolved—with fewer survival issues, for example—our thinking is no longer our tool, but rather we have become the tool of our thinking, and every thought creates friction, frustration, and emotion. This is why it is hard at first to see the difference between thoughts and emotions. When a thought triggers heat, heartbeat, or anything else in the body that is not yet even recognized as a specific feeling, it is already an emotion.

When we train our emotions, we first want to recognize the physiological change, such as heart rate, heat, tension. Then we use the emotions as a burst of energy before it changes the psychological and physiological thinking in our body. Since you cannot fight emotions, the only thing you can do is know better how your mind works and know how certain perceptions make your body react.

When you already feel an emotion, it is always good not to try to contain it and keep it in. It is better to let it go; otherwise, it will build up and hurt you. This is why a lot of the practice uses martial arts to let go of the tension. In fact, all the emotions come from fear—fear of not being, of losing our individuality, fear of pain, fear of dying. Fear is always covered by anger and sadness. Fear can be with an object or without object—anxiety. If it is anxiety, you can talk about it and find ways to work on the feeling, but if it comes from an object, you need to see if you are able to confront the object of your fear or learn to live with it. This process needs to be accompanied by a sage, your teacher or master; otherwise, it will bring you to sadness or anger or both. This is why in Daoism they say that only once you accept death can you actually live. Death is a process of life. It makes living easier and more enjoyable. The big thing of emotional practice is that since emotions are in the body, we can do something about them.

> *All spiritual practice has two concepts. First, you have to be there; you have to be present. Second, you have to accept death and confront fear.*

This is why in our practice, as well in the martial arts, it is very important to train the two concepts above.

Innate and acquired Jing

You have two types of Jing. One is energy given by your Jing, your essence that was there when you were created as a human being. The essence of your father and mother meet; when it works, the Yuan Shen (spirit) makes a spark. The two Jings create a third Jing in which you already have energy, the desire to live, and what was given by your parents (good or bad). This is innate Jing before you are born. There is nothing you can do about it. Then you have post-heaven Jing, which is energy that you acquire and that you can build. Let's say your parents gave you very poor Jing, which means your countdown to death is very short. Each time you are tired in the day means your acquired Jing is has been used up. You carry on your activities, using the innate Jing, and you make your little counter go faster. You grow older faster.

All you have to do is build up abundant acquired Qi through training so that you never have to use the innate Qi. Say you just have two dollars in the bank (poor Jing) but you never spend it because people offer you enough to live on; you really don't care if your innate Jing is good or bad since there are ways to protect it and never use it. This is the training.

Daoist immortality

With your innate Jing, you are at your best when you reach the age of 30—and then it goes downhill! But after a few years' training, the acquired energy makes you better every day, countering natural cell degeneration. So the postnatal work through your practice will counter the evolution of your prenatal Qi, allowing you to be in good health and strong until you die. Immortality does not mean living forever, but living a healthy life until your death and, as a result of good health, a prolonged life.

The mind

Your thinking is a big problem because it completely overrides your other perceptions. Everything you see is interpreted inside. There is only inside perception. Everybody sees their own little world. Very quickly, when you know how your mind works, you will be able to balance the Shen.

The mind has four aspects. Two aspects are the basis of who you are—the instinctive aspect, animalistic survival (Po), and a very spiritual soul aspect (Hun).

The first thing that happens when the Jing of the parents meet with a spark and you are created is that the Po takes this energy and makes it incarnate into life. Once the Po is there, for a couple of weeks it does not understand that it is separated from its mother. Then it separates. The Hun, the soul, will stay with you all your life and is the closest thing to the God-like idea we have of things (messages, intuition, divine aspect of our mind, Yang).

These two aspects are fixed on a vertical line when you are three years old. Then you start to act (Zhi aspect) and later the child starts to think of what he does—this is the Yi, the intellectual aspect. This horizontal line of Yi and Po is planning and action. These four aspects form the human, Shen process.

On these two main axes with four directions you have diagonals crossing through the center of the directions, and these determine different aspects of your behavior as a human being. Each part of the mind is associated with different qualities, capacities, emotions.

Your mind comprises your spiritual aspect, your survival aspect, your thinking, your intellectual aspect, and your realization, or doing, aspect.

If you already know this in detail through your practice, you will recognize that some aspects work for you and some do not, and you will be better able to see where the emotion is coming from and what you need to train. The more you know about yourself, the more you see things coming from afar. It is as if someone is hiding behind a wall to scare you. If you are not expecting it, you can be startled, but if you know he is hiding, it will not have the same effect!

The practice is about learning how we function, so that you can go *with* that and not against it. This is the famous Wu Wei, non-action—actually not going against, being non-resistant. For this we need to work each one of our aspects in order to differentiate very clearly what we do. The mind, the emotions, breathing, body—there is a very systematic approach for each, and this way you do not get everything confused.

When you feel that something is wrong, you have a choice: deal with it and confront it, or don't. If you don't, it will confront you later, and it will be a lot worse because you will no longer be in charge.

The problems you have to face are a little like the trash you have to take out every day. If you let it pile up, it will not disappear but it will start smelling bad, and then it will require a lot of effort to get rid of it. But if you decide to do it daily, it is much more manageable and you stay in control.

The three minds

In our school we say we have three minds. First, there is the one in your head, commenting on everything that you confuse with you. We call this "the one we think we are" (the ego). Sometimes you act in a particular way and do not recognize yourself. This means there is something else! Furthermore, if you are commenting, it means you have something on which to comment! This means there is something behind. The second mind is who you really are. You can connect to this by training, but we need our mental mind in our daily life. These two are pretty much who we are: something absolute and something practical.

But then there is a third one: the one you pretend to be—all the different personalities you have, depending on who you are interacting with. You do not behave in the same with your family, partner, friends, work colleagues, and so on. This is the one we can get rid of! The more fake characters you have, the more you will have a bad feeling inside and the more you will have emotions that come from nowhere. The more you behave and act the way you think you are, the better you feel, but you will also have the real and deeper problems that you have to face. It is the same with dreams which you can experience in so many different ways, but you always have a few recurring things expressed in different ways. These are the real issues. There is less friction in your mind between all the different roles, and suddenly your Shen Gong training is much more clear.

Shen Gong: Mind training

Mind training has nothing to do with breathing (Nei Dan). It is looking at your thinking. First, you have to be silent, not moving, and aligned. All you have to do is close your eyes and look. In the beginning it makes no sense, but after a while your mind stops bringing up uninteresting information and starts to bring useful information. And if it doesn't, we have tools to help the mind focus in a direction or to bring the mind towards a resolution. This first step of looking at your mind should be done every day. Gradually it will bring more interesting things, but it is a process.

The mind cannot be controlled but it can be tamed. First, however, we have to make friends with it, just like a wild animal. But there is a long time of adapting, especially since most of us have never been taught to do this. All of these years of not cleaning the mind have brought chaos. The mind can only do one thing at a time. If you are still and only looking at your mind, you cannot be bored. If you are bored, it is because you are not looking at your mind. This is the same with the breathing. This is why if you find enthusiasm in the practice, you will never be bored because you will be focusing on the exercise and nothing else.

Sometimes the exercise can go by very fast and other days it seems to last forever, depending on the way you focus. In that sense, time does not exist! The process of time that we have in the mind or intellectually is not true. Time does not exist: you can experience only moments, in the past, present or future. And the line of time created by your mind is the brain trying to put all the points of moments together. When you wait for a train to start to move, there is not a moment when you see it start. It is either stopped or going. It is a point—you can never grab it. When you practice, time disappears because you are in who you are and not on a linear succession of points. Who you really are is not in the web of time; it is somewhere else.

Boredom is the first defense mechanism of your ego. The ego wants to control, and if the ego does not understand what is going on, it will get bored. When you see something beautiful for the first time, such as a beautiful painting, first you just have the feeling, but then you need to explain, give yourself reasons for what you like about it. The ego wants to control by understanding everything. In Da Xuan, the Big Secret, what is hidden—but only because light has not been shone upon it—is actually our mind. Looking at the mind starts the process of bringing light to the hidden secret.

To start the exercise you must sit down, remaining absolutely still and with silent breathing, close your eyes, and look at your mind. Once again, if you feel the exercise is making you doze off, sit on the edge of the chair so that you must keep your balance. This is true introspection: trying to understand yourself, by yourself.

The second level of Shen Gong is looking at yourself in action. Following a lot of introspective meditation, it is very interesting to take a few minutes every evening to look at your day and make a summary of your actions and behavior, and what you were satisfied or unsatisfied with. Most interestingly, you can notice the discrepancy between your values, how you wish to act, and what you really did. It is important to have the two visions of yourself— the psychological, introspective aspect and the behavioral aspect. I look at the values and rules I have with others. "Others" means me plus at least one other person. If I don't have my own values, or never took time set them up, they will have been established by the education I received, and I go with them and react accordingly. But if I take time to look at this, now as an adult and independent, a lot of the rules I have are not necessarily what I think today and I need to make the distinction.

Then I look at myself in action with society (me plus at least one other). You look at how you act and whether that is in accordance with the values you have established or far from them. For instance, you might have ecological values and believe that we should take care of our planet. You have your containers for recycling and regular rubbish, but in fact you see yourself throwing anything in whatever trash just because it takes more time to sort the items.

So this is the difference between what you think you should do and what you are actually doing. One part of this only concerns yourself and the other concerns you with other people. Together, these are the four levels of training:

I train to clarify the relationship I have with myself.

I train to look at myself in action.

I look at my values and what I have been brought up with.

I look at the way I interact with society.

As you can see in these four levels of training, one half concerns me and the other half concerns the world. Training just for yourself is OK as long as you live in retreat in a monastery in the mountains. Otherwise, it just does not work. This is why many of the ways developed by people who have been in retreat do not adapt to our lives. They do not offer the appropriate tools.

First, this introspection aspect requires looking at your mind with the Shen Gong exercises. This is not easy! It feels like a waste of time since the mind is not flexible. But if you do it enough and on a daily basis, things will come out. As long as you sit down and do it, this will be beneficial. There is no bad Shen Gong, even if you comment on your exercise, thinking it is useless. You cannot look for results but just find time to do it. And slowly it will become something else. The mind will give you information and then you find enthusiasm.

When you train your body, it will become strong and relaxed enough to stay still for a long time, and when you do the Nei Dan (breathing work), your emotions and energy are strong enough to sustain your attention. The big problem with attention is that at some point your mind wanders off. This is not just because you are bored but also because you lack energy to stay focused. So you have to train Nei Dan to have more energy and for the body to feel stronger.

The static postures are a good way to train you to align your body. We start by standing, but it can be done sitting or lying down. All the static training is best done standing up: it will more easily create Qi and give you grounding. You generate Yang energy very readily with the static positions, and this Yang energy will be felt easily because you are not using it for motion. If you keep a slight tension in your fingers and your arms open, this will also train the tendons in a specific way. It also makes the fascia develop in specific ways to protect the cavities of the body. The Yang energy transforms the Yin structure and makes the body fuller. It is a way to quieten the noises from your head but also any kind of tension in the body. Then you start to be aligned and everything is possible.

When and where to train

Depending on your rhythm, you will find some moments of the day or night when the mind is at its most quiet. That would be the ideal time to train at first. Very quickly, however, when the training becomes more familiar, it can be done at any time. The same applies to the places you train. Choosing a place you like because of its scenery or peaceful aspect can be helpful at first because it feeds you emotionally. But in fact it has nothing to do with the quality of energy, because energy is the same everywhere, whether you train in a small cubicle or the Grand Canyon. The difference is just the emotion and intent you put into the training.

During Shen Gong you close your eyes to watch your mind. To train attention if you are lacking it, however, you can train with your eyes open, keeping them set on a very simple object, not too small and not too big. You keep your focus on this object during the whole exercise. As soon as you realize that your mind wanders, you come back to the center—that is, the object. This is called "fitness of attention," but it has nothing directly to do with Shen Gong. You are just training one of the tools here. Then you use the stamina you developed to look at your mind during Shen Gong training.

In this book we have presented most of what makes our practice a practice: the different aspects, the feeling, and what you are looking for—for real.

> *Do not be fooled by nebulous, complicated writings. It should be simple, because this practice has been developed by very practical people. It should be usable and easy to understand.*

Questions and Answers

1. Are there any medical or psychological conditions that would made practicing the exercises in this book inadvisable? With a master teacher, can almost any condition be helped by practice?

There are no problems with these practices. The only concern is that you may feel stuck or be confronted by questions that can only be solved by a teacher. You need to have a teacher at some point. If you are unbalanced already when you start the exercises, the practice will help you, but you need to find a teacher to go deeper and balance your mind.

2. What are the shadows you often mention? Is the ego in fact made up of these shadows?

Each part of the Shen has shadows. Yi has ego and overthinking, Zhi has fear of new or other people, Hun has confusion and apathy, Po has preconceived thinking and attachment. All of these are shadows, more or less developed, depending our Ba Zi and our history.

3. Is Qigong a more modern term for Nei Dan and Nei Gong?

Yes, I use Nei Gong for Jing (and Wai Gong for body) and Nei Dan for breath.

Case Studies

Case 1: You do not need to believe

One of my students was an active duty army officer, very stressed, very "on edge." We had mutual friends and they persuaded him to meet me. He talked to me about his problems—his lack of sleep and general tension. It was clear to me that his Qi was blocked by emotional tension. I knew he did not believe the Qi and Daoist concepts, but I told him that I would make him do some "breath training" so that he would have more stamina. He loved the idea. After a month of the Nei Dan regimen, he could sleep better and was even smiling a lot. Now he wanted to know more, to learn more. He is still a student today and he does Shen Gong and Nei Dan every day.

Case 2: You do not need time

A woman came to see me after having her third child. She was a good friend of one of my female students. She wanted to train but couldn't imagine how to get more free time—she had none already. I taught her Nei Dan—Yuan Nei Dan, in fact—to do throughout her busy day, for minutes at a time. She did this and felt so much energy that she could take care of her kids, her job, and her husband…and still feel fine at the end of the day. Once her children were older, she was able to start a real practice, but she achieved a great basis with the "moments practice." She still practices today.

Case 3: You do not need to be young

An older lady came to the training on crutches. She was 84 years old and had been doing another form of meditation. With Nei Dan and some Wai Gong—training every day of course—she was soon walking without problem and went back traveling at 85 and a half. She trained gently but every day, coming back to me regularly, getting more of the teachings, and training her body and her mind.